We can't afford to underestimate the importance of doing relationships well. I've seen this area repeatedly make or break people. We in the Hillsong United Band call Jeanne our "American Mum." As only she can deliver it, *UNCENSORED* gives practical advice on real issues that many people are too scared to address. It's about time a book like this was written!

—JOEL HOUSTON
HILLSONG UNITED BAND
SYDNEY, AUSTRALIA

I consider Jeanne Mayo a trusted and respected friend. Like myself, she has invested her life into impacting emerging youth cultures. She embodies Emerson's quote, "The years will teach you what the days will never know." That's why she brings nearly 4 decades of valuable in-the trench youth ministry experience to her writing of UNCENSORED. I recommend the book highly to anyone courageous enough to value a straight-talk approach to dating, friendship, and sex.

—JOSH MCDOWELL
INTERNATIONAL SPEAKER AND AUTHOR
PRESIDENT, JOSH MCDOWELL MINISTRIES

The strongest endorsement I can give for Uncensored is that I desperately wish I'd read it when I was a teenager—this is, simply, the most courageous, true, and practical book I've ever read on romantic relationships. In fact, this book is so profoundly practical that I'm right now thinking about Jeanne's wisdom in the context of my own marriage—her focus is Jesus, and her insights are treasure. I can't wait to give this book to my daughters because I can't think of a better friend than Jeanne to come alongside them as they navigate their own intimate journeys.

—RICK LAWRENCE
EXECUTIVE EDITOR OF GROUP MAGAZINE
AUTHOR OF JESUS-CENTERED YOUTH MINISTRY

Unhealthy and distorted romantic desire can capture a person early in life and cause pain for years to come. Today's youth and young adult culture will find the pages of *Uncensored* to be both a friend and a weapon in this battlefront. I recommend it highly.

—REGGIE DABBS
INTERNATIONAL YOUTH COMMUNICATOR

Jeanne Mayo has almost single-handedly taken youth ministry from a feebly furnished back room to the forefront of the church. Anytime she puts pen to paper we must take notice! This book comes at a critical time—ignore it at your regret.

—JUDAH SMITH
YOUTH PASTOR
CITY CHURCH, SEATTLE, WASHINGTON

Jeanne Mayo is an incredible communicator to young people (and she's funny)! Her insights will help you make wise choices and live out the great plan God has for your life! I recommend her new book, *Uncensored,* as a "must read."

—PHIL DOOLEY
HILLSONG CHURCH YOUTH PASTOR
HILLSONG CHURCH, SYDNEY, AUSTRALIA

Jeanne Mayo takes on the issues of dating and sexuality with a unique balance of compassion and fearlessness. She not only speaks to young people, but for them. The vibrant personality and straight-forward approach that have made her a national resource on youth ministry make this book one you will want to have and use.

—EARL CREPS, PH.D.
AUTHOR, SPEAKER, AND DIRECTOR OF DOCTOR OF MINISTRY PROGRAM
ASSEMBLIES OF GOD THEOLOGICAL SEMINARY

UNCENSORED

DATING, FRIENDSHIPS, AND SEX

YOU THINK YOU KNOW...
BUT YOU HAVE NO IDEA.

JEANNE MAYO

HARRISON HOUSE
TULSA, OKLAHOMA

**FOR THOSE WHO DARE TO ASK
THE TOUGH QUESTIONS**

THANKS

TO SAM, the greatest husband, protector, and hero a gal could ever have. ♡

To my firstborn son, Josh, and my "daughter-in-love," Monica, who made the gutsy relational choices to create a "marriage kissed by eternity."

To the "one and only Justin Mayo," who walks with more relational favor on his life than anyone I've ever known (and has more fun in the process).

To Mike & Diane, Kenn & Kathy, my sis Barb, Doc Boyer & Elaine, Dan & Megan, Paul & Karen, and Ray & Claudia: without your prayers and sacrifice none of this would be happening now. Thanks for believing in the dream.

To the team in Atlanta that has healed me by their unselfish friendship and brought my heart back to life: Jordan, Dave, Stefanie, Alex, Laurie, Judy, Missy, and Company.

To the people I so cherish in Master's Commission Atlanta and OXYGEN: Thank you for giving me the privilege of being a "mom" and a "coach." You make each day worthwhile.

To my soulmate, Joani, who has fulfilled my secret longing for a "girl-friend" who both loves to have fun and loves teenagers.

To my treasured Paula & John and Erin & Aaron, who courageously dared to guard their hearts from cheap compromises and are now redefining "marriage" at its best. And to my "Annie," who relentlessly refuses to "settle."

To Michael & Dru for living a life of passionate unselfishness and blazing Christ-likeness.

To Lee & Janie for remaining in my life and redefining the term, "lifelong friends."

To the champions I now fondly call "The Cadre" who have given my life so much fresh passion, meaning, and fire that I'm motivated to "finish the race with the wind in my face."

And to the thousands of young adults and teenagers who have been my cherished teachers on relationships through the years.

To all of you, I owe you far more than letters on this page. Thank you, my friends. You have marked my life forever—I will never, ever forget.

TABLE OF

CONTENTS

INTRODUCTION

SCRAWLED PATHETICALLY ON THE JAIL WALLS were Cody's last words, "Hailey, I will always love you." They were a chilling backdrop to the limp, dead body that was hanging from the jail ceiling right in front of them. Brokenhearted from a relationship gone bad, Cody had committed a senseless crime. He would have been out of jail only 3 days later. There would have been more friends…more girlfriends. But somehow, Cody couldn't see past the gaping rip in his own heart. He took his own life late one night, and left, as his legacy, only six words on the jail wall: "Hailey, I will always love you."

The uncensored power of relationships had left its mark on another human life. What had caused this ultimate desperation? How could the American sport we call "dating" crescendo to a suicide scene? Years later, as Cody's youth leader and friend, I'm still not sure I have the answers. I only know one thing for sure: CS Lewis was right when he said, "The only place free from the dangers of love is hell itself."

I've worked with college students and teenagers for many years. And with no hesitation, I firmly believe that relationships, both friendship and dating ones, are the single most powerful influence in their lives. Time and time again, I have reminded young adults I care about, "Show me your friends and I will show you your future." And yet our internal "longing for belonging" seems to often overpower common sense and reason in the lives of even some of the sharpest and the best.

So *Uncensored* is a journal of sorts. I've chronicled some of my most important interactions with countless young adults and teenagers as we've sorted through questions on dating, friendship, and sex. Pretty hot topics, wouldn't you say? I've even tried to live up to our title of "Uncensored" by including some candid chapters that most Christian books don't dare to tackle. *I'm either 'gutsy' or stupid—you decide!*

I guess as much as anything, *Uncensored* is my written rejection of the church world's TRT ("Typical Religious Talk"). While religious leaders piously babble about theology and doctrine, young adults living in the real world face mounting questions about relationships in their life: How do you build friendships that really last? How do you breakup without falling apart? How do relationships play into predicting your future? How do you deal with the touchy area of "solo sex"? And how do you maintain your personal integrity in a sex-saturated society?

My friends often smile over my countless one-liners (fondly termed "Mayoism's"), which you'll see scattered heavily through-out these pages. Some are fun like "Puppy love leads to a dog's life"; while others just cause you to think, like "Right choices eventually bring right emotions." Whatever their slant, I include them as road markers to help navigate the exciting but challenging paths of friendship, dating, and sex.

Granted, you'll probably never find yourself so tormented over a relationship gone bad that suicide will be a serious option. Thank- ~~At least I sure hope you don't.~~ fully, Cody is a painful exception. But if you live long enough, I promise that you will sometimes find yourself in a relational "jail" of sorts—one you will create by some of your own friendship choices.

So grab some java and let's hang out together for a while as you make your way through the pages of this book. After all, we're dealing with some pretty important topics. Life without friendships would be pretty blah and empty; and life without the opposite sex would be minus one of the most exciting roller coaster rides imaginable. So allow me the privilege of making this fun-filled journey with you. We'll have a great time together, I promise. And then, as you conclude the final page, you'll be left on your own again to make your own personal relational decisions. Those decisions will ultimately be some of the most important "pens" in the writing of the "life chapters" you are about to experience.

And that, my friend, is the *Uncensored* truth.

Lovingly honored to be in your life,

THE SECRET TO FUN DATING

THE POISON THAT WILL KILL YOUR DATING LIFE

WHERE PLAYBOY AND I AGREE

THE SURE WAY TO BE ATTRACTIVE TO THE OPPOSITE SEX

BREAKING UP WITHOUT FALLING APART

10 THINGS GIRLS WISH GUYS KNEW

12 THINGS
GUYS WISH GIRLS KNEW.....

Welcome to the
    Olympic sport we
call 'dating'
American

SECTION 1

DATING

THE DATING MYTH
WE ALL WANT TO BELIEVE

WANTED: FEMALE CONTROL FREAKS

R-RATED
DATING ADVICE FROM
THE SCRIPTURES

"IN THE LAST 20 YEARS, WE HAVE NOT GONE THROUGH A SEXUAL REVOLUTION AS MUCH AS A REVOLUTION IN OUR SEARCH FOR INTIMACY."

—ANSON MOUNT

CO-AUTHOR OF THE "PLAYBOY PHILOSOPHY"

Chapter 01

WHERE PLAYBOY AND I AGREE

I'M DEEPLY COMMITTED in my relationship with Jesus Christ. So I surprised myself the day I decided that I agreed with part of the "Playboy Philosophy." I stumbled onto the info innocently. (No, I wasn't browsing through Playboy!) I was doing a talk on our search for intimacy and found Anson Mount's quote. His credentials made his words even more significant. As the coauthor of the notorious "Playboy Philosophy," his observation was surprisingly right on the money.

He stated, "In the last 20 years, we have not gone through a sexual revolution as much as a revolution in our search for intimacy." I've worked with teenagers and university students for lots of years. I've been part of the "morning after" discussions more times than I can count. But let me tell you one of my biggest conclusions.

Many people today share their *bodies* because they are afraid to share *themselves*.

Countless surveys have been done on all of this. One I recently reviewed included thousands of teenagers and unmarried people. They were asked to select six things that were most important to them from a list of twenty choices. Their overwhelming first choice (67 percent) was "a close, intimate relationship." Sex only made it to number six on the list.

A HUNGRY NEED IS A DANGEROUS NEED.

Remember hearing about a guy in the Bible named Esau? He wasn't exactly a rocket scientist. You see, in Genesis 25 we find out that he got so hungry that he agreed to sell his birthright to his brother for a bowl of soup. (Side note: The birthright was a big deal in Old Testament days. It basically was a guy's ticket to blessing, prosperity, and everything in his future he might need.)

What's the principle we learn from poor old Esau? It's an important one, my friend, so get ready to think hard when you read the next sentence: **A "hungry" need is a dangerous need.**

Let me translate that one for you. We all have "hungry emotional needs" in our lives. Some of us are "hungry" to be appreciated. Some of us are "hungry" to be liked and valued. Some of us are "hungry" to belong to someone and feel special. The list goes on and on.

But when a certain emotional need is raw and "hungry," we are all capable of doing really stupid things to fill it up (like trading off our spiritual birthright for a bowl of soup). How stupid is stupid?

HERE'S MY "STUPID ANONYMOUS" LIST:

- Stupid is giving away your body in hopes of holding on to a relationship.

- Stupid believes someone when they tell you, "You're the only one I've done this with."

- Stupid is thinking that 90 seconds of sexual pleasure will be an answer to gnawing emotional junk on the inside.

- Stupid is not realizing that true character is who you are in the dark.

- Stupid is forgetting that the very thing you give away in order to keep a person will ultimately be the very thing that contributes to your losing them. After all, now you'll be conquered and just like everybody else.

normal ≠ attractive

Another famous guy named Rollo Mayo agrees that "a hungry need is a dangerous need." He says, "Today, there is so much use of the body as a substitute for emotional intimacy. It's much easier to jump into bed with somebody than it is to share your fears, your *so true...* hopes, your dreams…all the things that go on inside a person's true, emotional self. Because the body becomes a sort of buffer, the pursuit of genuine and lasting intimacy gets short-circuited through the sexual act. Sadly, most people never experience true intimacy with the other person."

"So let's go get married!" I can hear some relational dummy mumbling to himself. No, Sweetheart, that's not going to fix the emotional vacuum. Only hard, honest work on yourself (over time) can do that. Why? Let me reword it one last time for you.

If you need to date or be married to feel fulfilled or loved, you are not ready to date or to marry. The very things in your life that make these needs so big will become the problem in any signifi-cant relationship.

So what's my answer? Why don't you read the chapter titled, "The Dating Myth We All Want To Believe." But let me give you its bottom-line principle: If you try to find intimacy with another person before doing the hard work of achieving a sense of identity on your own, all your relationships will become a painful attempt to complete yourself.

It's another one of those "uncensored answers." I'm not saying it's easy. I'm just saying it's right. So get to work on yourself. And in the meantime, try not to trade anything in your life for a bowl of soup!

"HOW MUCH YOU PUT INTO A DATING RELATIONSHIP DETERMINES HOW MUCH IT WILL HURT WHEN IT ENDS."

—JUSTIN LOOKADOO

Chapter

02

THE SECRET TO FUN DATING

DATING IS OBVIOUSLY A PRETTY FUN PROPOSITION. That's why it's such a big deal in our culture. But dating can also be pretty brutal. So I'm about to share a secret with you that will help shape your dating outlook in some pretty amazing ways. It might sound a little harsh, but it's a fact that will be huge in keeping your dating fun.

Could you do me a favor? What I'm about to say is really important. So how about turning off the TV and focusing in on this page for a minute? Ready? Here goes…

If you're in high school or early college and you're dating, it won't last.

Did you catch those last three words? It won't last. *Don't get defensive— Just keep reading.*

I mean, one of you is going to get the "Dear John" (or "Joanie") speech. You're going to breakup. It will end. And somebody's going to be really sad.

Sound depressing? Only if you don't understand why I want you to face this statistical truth. You see, if you don't get a hold of this fact, dating will rip you up one side and down the other. It's only when you face the brutal truth that 99.9 percent of all dating relationships do not last that you become really free to enjoy this whole process.

That's why this realization is so huge in helping your dating relationships to stay fun.

IF YOU DON'T REALIZE THAT YOUR DATING WON'T LAST, YOU WILL GIVE AWAY FAR TOO MUCH EMOTIONAL, MENTAL, AND PHYSICAL ENERGY TO KEEP IT GOING.

51% of teenage marriages end in divorce before the age of 24.[1]

I know what you're thinking. Go ahead and say it. You think you're the exception to the statistics and that the dating relationship you're in will quite possibly lead you to the wedding altar. Think again, my friend.

I'm a woman on a mission to get this truth through your head. Say what you will, the statistics are against you. It won't last. Why is that so important for you to know? (This next sentence is important, too, so work with me here. Come on. Concentrate!)

If you don't realize that your dating won't last, you will give away far too much emotional, mental, and physical energy to keep it going. You see, if you think that the relationship you're in is meant to last for a lifetime, you will do really stupid things to keep it alive. (Did I say, "really stupid"?)

That's where sex comes in. You've seen it before: one of the people in a dating relationship feels that sex will glue them back together if and when they are starting to slowly come apart. So they do "what-ever it takes" to have a few minutes of false intimacy. But when *which at the moment, feels really real.* they realize this dating relationship really isn't going to last, it's really much easier. They play it smart. Why would you give yourself away to someone you are going to breakup with? (Or worse yet, someone who is going to breakup with you?)

Too often, our society is in love with being in love. Why wouldn't we be? Almost every movie and song that crosses our paths make us think that romance is the answer to every need in our lives. But when you are "in love with love," you forget that **"puppy love often leads to a dog's life!"** (No barking necessary. I just want you to get the point.)

Dating is supposed to be fun. Believe me, I've worked with young adults for plenty of years, and I really enjoy being the "divine match-maker"! But the fun is short-lived when the couple puts too much focus on their relationship. Let's weigh your options. Why not plug in your brain? When you realize that statistics tell you that it won't last, you can relax and come at this dating thing with a much more balanced perspective. *Is this too soon in the book for me to be this honest?*

And when you do breakup (Notice that I said "when."), you come away from the relationship knowing more about yourself and about other people, and with a hundred great memories of fun, crazy things you did together. (That does not include taking naps together in the backseat of a car.)

Just let me tell you one more really important fact: How much you put into a dating relationship determines how much it will hurt when it ends.[2] So why pour your total mind, body, and soul into a relationship, knowing that you are merely making down payments on your own future pain? *and these payments can be pricey*

What did you just say? You muttered, "Because I love him (her), and we're different."

Get a grip, my friend. Go read this chapter again. Only when you really get this principle will your dating relationships leave you with more fun memories than painful ones. Remember it as the three-word secret for happy dating perspective: It won't last. That's the uncensored truth that will keep fun (and balance) in your dating life.

And what if you choose to ignore this "secret"? It's a free society. I only have one closing comment: Happy barking!

This stuff really works!

A SURE WAY TO BE ATTRACTIVE TO THE OPPOSITE SEX

WELCOME TO THE "MAYO DATING SERVICE." So you just proved me right. Thanks. I told my publisher that you'd turn to this chapter fast! After all, the title is a hot button for most of our culture. At any rate, let's get down to business.

I'd like to talk to you about a law that went into motion right after the first human beings were formed in the Garden of Eden. That's right. This principle has been around since good ol' Adam and Eve showed up on the scene. Remember how God told them they could eat from absolutely any tree in the entire garden? Except one, that is. Introducing: "The Law of Forbidden Fruit."

You don't have to be a Bible scholar to know what happened next. Adam and Eve decided that the one tree they *really* wanted to eat from just happened to be the one and only tree God told them they couldn't have. What a coincidence. And the rest is history.

What's my point? Since the beginning of time, our human nature has been attracted to what we couldn't quite have or do. Not you?  Think again. Just stop to realize how unusually attractive food gets to you the day after you tell yourself you're on a diet. Or think of the "Do not touch" signs you occasionally see on a wall that's just been freshly painted. Stare at that sign long enough, and you'll find yourself with a crazy desire to touch the wall. (Just because they told you that you couldn't.) It's the way our twisted human nature works. Blame it all on Adam and Eve.

So, how's that relate to dating and romance? It does in a huge way. A lot of single individuals make themselves incredibly unattractive by coming across as too eager, too easily interested, and too quick to jump if a dating opportunity comes along.

Once in a relationship, these same people often hold on too tightly to the other person, sending signals that they are "in this thing forever—no matter what the cost." This kind of selfless commitment is great for marriage, but *not* for dating. In the dating world, it sends a quiet signal that you're not worth much—that you can be walked on, taken for granted, or mistreated but you'll still hang around.

Wrong move. People are attracted to others who come across as self-confident, fulfilled, and even a little hard-to-get. Let me help by giving you some more bottom lines. If you do a few simple things, you help to make yourself pretty irresistible.

This makes you "disposable"
- NOT valuable.

MAKING YOURSELF IRRESISTIBLE

DR. ELAINE WALSTER and other researchers talk in *Psychology Today* about an experiment they did along these lines with several hundred college men. Big, mind-blowing discovery! Guys said they liked women who came across as a little hard-to-get. (Translated: They liked girls who were a little mysterious—girls who seemed untouchable.)

But the data in the experiment broke down after the first date. You see, with half the men on the first date, the women were told to be slightly detached and elusive. With the other half, the girls were told to be friendly and warm almost immediately. Guess which of the two groups got the highest demand for a second date. Just the opposite from what the guys *thought* they wanted. That's right. The girls who got asked out for a second date were the girls who projected emotional warmth and friendliness on that very first date. (Quick word to the wise: "Emotional warmth" is not the same as making out or going to bed with someone. That's not being "warm." That's being "easy".)

Just keep reading

What were the findings from *Psychology Today?* Drum roll, please. The study concluded that the most appealing person to date is the one who outwardly projects herself (himself) as slightly hard-to-get. Yet, once on the date itself, she (he) projects warmth and fun from the very beginning. Put those two attributes together, and you've made yourself really appealing to the opposite sex. The trick is to be warm, though, without coming across like you are totally caught or conquered. Things that come too easy just don't seem to keep our attention.[7]

Ask an honest friend how you come across.

So let me summarize. If you want to be amazingly attractive to people of the opposite sex, just combine "The Law of Forbidden Fruit" *(You always want to date the person who doesn't act like they would immediately jump into your arms)* along with "The Law of Human Attraction" *(People like people who like them).* Put those two irresistible forces together, and I promise you, your attractiveness quota will go up. Way up. *↑UP*

Now, I'm not promising you'll be dating next week…or next month…or even next year. But I will promise you that the combining of these two laws will make you very attractive to the opposite sex…when the time is right.

DON'T BE LIKE KEITH RUFF

EVER HEARD OF KEITH RUFF? His story was told in the Los Angeles Times. The headline read, "Man Spends $20,000 Trying to Win the Hand of Girl Who Continues to Say 'No.'" Keith obviously didn't know about our formula for human attraction. In attempts to get a certain young woman to like him, he spent over $20,000 on gifts for her. Let me make you laugh with a few of them:

- A Learjet, placed on leased standby at the airport, "in case she wanted to ride around."

- Over 3,000 flowers.

- Musicians to serenade her.

- A clown to amuse her younger brother.

- A guy dressed up like Prince Charming who delivered a glass slipper.

- And for her parents, a stepladder, "so they could look at our relation-ship from a different angle."

Obviously, Keith Ruff invested a ton of money on some unnamed girl. But there was only one problem: The girl refused to even go out on one date with the guy! Apparently nobody ever told him about **Sorry** "The Law of Forbidden Fruit." So the next time you're tempted to **Keith!** play it too easy, remind yourself, "I'm no Keith Ruff!"

Let me close out this chapter by offering one final piece of advice. All relationships ultimately go through tough times when breakups occur. When this happens, don't freak out. If the other person gives signals of wanting to call it quits, don't cheapen yourself by desperately trying to hold on. Strive to come across poised, secure, and equally independent. If you begin to grovel and act like your world is coming to an end, you're only pushing the other person further away from you. But if you remain confident and calm on the outside (even though you may be crushed on the inside), you're making yourself much more appealing to the other person. Your odds of having a "happily ever after" ending go way up.

Give these ideas a try and I promise you'll be more attractive to the opposite sex. Even if you disagree with my approach, they sure beat Keith Ruff's tactics. Besides that, you'll save $20,000 in the process!

"IT IS ONLY WHEN WE
NO LONGER
COMPULSIVELY
NEED SOMEONE
THAT WE CAN
HAVE A REAL
RELATIONSHIP
WITH THEM."

—ANTHONY STORR

Chapter 04

THE DATING MYTH WE ALL WANT TO BELIEVE

It's the dating myth and fairytale we all really want to believe. There's only one problem. It's a big, painful lie.

What am I talking about? It's the aching belief that "Mr. or Miss Right" is going to enter our lives. Then they will suddenly make our whole life incredibly happy and fulfilled. It's what counselors would call "The Compulsion for Completion." And whether we admit it or not, we all are affected to some degree by this deceptive fairytale. We want someone to enter our lives who will give us a meaningful identity and make us feel deeply whole on the inside.

But here's the uncensored truth: There are no shortcuts to personal growth and wholeness. **If you try to complete yourself through another person before you do the hard work of cultivating strong self-esteem**

> on your own, every relationship will eventually end with disappoint-
> ment and pain. Why? Because every relationship will be an uncon-
> scious attempt to complete yourself.

None of us like to feel alone. We do about anything to distract ourselves from that gnawing feeling in the pit of our stomachs. But in the middle of those times, we begin to buy into a toxic lie: "When I find the right person, my life will be complete." Too bad it's just not *Even if the movies say it is.* that easy. You see, the emptiness inside all of us is not a case of missing persons in our lives, but a case of incompleteness deep down in our own souls.

I can hear what you're thinking again. "Jeanne, you're sounding like a shrink! Back off and stay practical." But I *am* staying practical. Remember? The title of this book is *Uncensored*. Unless I shoot straight with you on this whole concept of your "compulsion for completion," you're going to finish the book as empty as you started it.

I see this whole nasty fairytale play out almost every day of my life. Because I work with teenagers and young adults, discussions on the "D word" (dating) are almost an everyday occurrence. Just recently I had someone in my office talking about the guy of her dreams that she had just begun dating. She excitedly told me how perfect he was. But midstream in our talk together, she became suddenly emotional. As I passed her the tissue box, I asked, "What's going on inside your head right now? I thought you were really crazy about this guy."

"I am, Jeanne," she answered back passionately. "I'm just afraid I'm going to mess this whole thing up and lose him like I've done in every other relationship." This girl went on to tell me how "Mr. Right" helped her to overcome her insecurities and her fears. "When I'm with him," she said softly, "I just feel more whole on the inside."

My heart dropped. The young lady I was talking with was sharp. But I didn't need to be Dr. Phil to know that she was heading for relational trouble. Why? Because like everyone else lacking a solid sense of personal wholeness, she was looking to another person to complete her identity. No wonder she was terrified of a breakup. Remember the Greek myth about "Pandora's Box"? Hidden inside the box were all the painful parts of Pandora that she was trying to avoid, the parts of her inner self that she was trying to bury. But it was all those hidden and buried parts that were giving Pandora trouble. Most people stop the story right there, but the important part is how the Greek myth ended.

You see, as those parts inside Pandora's box were exposed to the light, she made her way to the bottom of the box. What did she find there? She found what had been missing her whole life—*hope*. You see, when she took the time to explore all of the hidden pieces, she found the key to her own wholeness.

So let me walk you through a few simple steps that help you live in the bright light of God's truth, instead of staying deceived by a fairytale that will never deliver happiness to you. What should we call this? Maybe...

worth giving some time to

STEPS TO GET TO THE BOTTOM OF YOUR OWN "PANDORA'S BOX"

01. If you haven't achieved a solid sense of who you are on your own, you will ultimately fall into one of the two distortions that will sabotage all your relationships:

a. "I need this person to be truly complete." Or

b. "If this person needs me, I'll be complete."

Both of these thoughts are not only lies, but they also form an agonizing roadblock to your own personal happiness and wholeness. If you buy into either one of these subtle lies, you'll come up empty every time. It isn't anyone else's job to give

23

you a healthy identity or to make you whole. People in your life are meant to (share) it, not to (be) it.

So for starters, recognize these lies that sabotage your completeness and fight them when they try to enter your heart and head. No matter how real and right they may feel, I promise you they won't work.

02. **Have the guts to look at some of your personal hurts (little or big, past or present) and realize the impact they are having on your present life and relationships.** I think of myself as one of the most blessed, fortunate women in the world. I am married

I love you, Sam

to the greatest husband any woman could ask for, I have two extraordinary adult sons who sincerely love me, and now I have the most loving, caring daughter-in-love I could have ever dreamed possible. What more could a woman want?

But as I write this chapter, the Lord is faithful to bring one name to my mind from my recent past. Though I try to

And this wasn't even romantic

pretend the pain is not there, I still feel the sting of their self-centeredness and lack of authentic love for me. Even as I type this chapter, my eyes fill involuntarily with tears. Stink! I don't want to feel that pain anymore. (Always remember that the people you love the most have the capability of hurting you the deepest.)

unfortunately

What's my point? Pain doesn't just go away. It takes work to face it, journal on it, speak honestly when necessary, and refuse to simply bury it. I've learned that painful emotions I try to bury have a high rate of resurrection. You may wonder why dealing with your emotions is really necessary. After all, it makes us feel weak. God knows the world doesn't need another "Drama Queen" (or "King" for that matter).

But the purpose behind the process is to protect you from repeating the pain of your past in your present relationships. That may sound strange, but the truth is we use new relationships kind of like replacement parts for old hurts and losses (a parent, an ex-boyfriend, a mean boss, etc.). In my own case, I can honestly see now how buried pain is affecting my current relationships. Without realizing it (until about fifteen minutes ago), I am holding certain people at an "arm's length" away from me emotionally—kind of as a safeguard to protect my heart from repeating that kind of anguishing disappointment again.

How's that for being real?

"DON'T BE FOOLED BY ME. DON'T BE FOOLED BY THE FACE I WEAR. I WEAR A MASK.

I WEAR A THOUSAND MASKS—MASKS THAT I AM AFRAID TO TAKE OFF; AND NONE OF THEM ARE ME. PRETENDING IS AN ART THAT IS SECOND NATURE TO ME, BUT DON'T BE FOOLED. FOR MY SAKE, PLEASE DON'T BE FOOLED.

I GIVE THE IMPRESSION THAT I AM SECURE, THAT ALL IS SUNNY AND UNRUFFLED WITHIN ME AS WELL AS WITHOUT; THAT CONFIDENCE IS MY NAME AND COOLNESS IS MY GAME. THAT THE WATER IS CALM AND I AM IN COMMAND; THAT I NEED NO ONE. BUT PLEASE DON'T BELIEVE ME, PLEASE. MY SURFACE MAY SEEM SMOOTH, BUT MY SURFACE IS A MASK, MY EVER CHANGING AND EVER CONCEALING MASK.

WHO AM I, YOU MAY WONDER? I AM SOMEONE YOU KNOW VERY WELL. I AM EVERY MAN YOU MEET. I AM EVERY WOMAN YOU MEET. I AM RIGHT IN FRONT OF YOU. IN TRUTH, I PROBABLY AM YOU."

03. In gutsy honesty with yourself, figure out what masks you wear and begin to take them off. Abraham Maslow talked about how we all wear a mask. We all put up our guard, especially to protect ourselves from possible rejection. Maslow used a cool term, calling us "jellyfish in armor" who pretend to be something we really aren't.

- Years ago at a retreat, I published an open letter on this whole subject of masks. The author of the original poem is Charles C. Finn. But if we are all truly honest with ourselves, most any of us could have written it:

"Don't be fooled by me. Don't be fooled by the face I wear. I wear a mask.

"I wear a thousand masks—masks that I am afraid to take off; and none of them are me. Pretending is an art that is second nature to me, but don't be fooled. For my sake, please don't be fooled.

"I give the impression that I am secure, that all is sunny and unruffled within me as well as without; that confidence is my name and coolness is my game. That the water is calm and I am in command; that I need no one. But please don't believe me, please. My surface may seem smooth, but my surface is a mask, my ever changing and ever concealing mask.

"*Who am I,* you may wonder? I am someone you know very well. I am every man you meet. I am every woman you meet. I am right in front of you. In truth, I probably am you."[3]

04. **Take responsibility for running your own life—for controlling your own destiny.** Put yourself in the driver's seat when it comes to becoming more and more whole on the inside. Don't wait on other people to help you feel more secure or whole about yourself. It's your life. Now kick yourself *in the rear* out of neutral and own it!

It's been said that most of us plan more carefully for a Christmas party than we do for our own love-life. How true. And when it comes to achieving internal wholeness and building a solid self-image, we all want something to just zap us. We want it to come like magic—either through a significant relationship or maybe even through having a very spiritual person pray with us.

But let me level with you. None of that stuff lasts—not for the long term. That's why the thinking that another earthly relationship can make you complete is so suicidal. Healthy self-worth and emotional wholeness only come from hard work on your part and from healthy choices, repeated over time. Sorry. I know that's not what you want to hear. But that really is the uncensored truth. George Bernard Shaw had it right: "Hell is to drift, heaven is to steer." So start steering, my friend!

05. **Allow Jesus Christ to become the centerpiece of your search for wholeness.** He and He alone can be trusted to fill the vacuums in your heart, to heal the wounds, and to consistently be the kind of Friend we all yearn for. Just like Corrie Ten Boom, the famous holocaust survivor, once said, "When Jesus is all you have, Jesus will be all you need."

I realize that this book will float in a thousand different directions. I also realize that some people reading it may choose never to explore the truth of this fifth vital step. But though churches and people may have failed you miserably, Jesus Christ never will.

Truth can be a scary thing

I'm not asking you to become a certain "religion." Christianity isn't about religious rules. At its heart, it is about a relationship—a personal relationship between you and Christ. I only want you to know the abundant life Jesus Christ brings to you when, in kid-like faith, you ask Him to come inside your life and forgive you for all the junk that separates you from Him. Then, by a simple choice of your will, you *choose* to make Him your Best Friend, Lord, and Master.

Why do I say all this? Because Jesus Christ is the only Person who can really consistently meet our "compulsion for completion." Even the best earthly relationships will fail us from time to time. Every single one of us needs to feel a deep sense of personal significance. This need is woven into the deepest parts of who we are. Jesus Christ alone can be counted on to genuinely love us unconditionally and fulfill our deepest longings consistently. No amount of money, relationships, beauty, success, or fame can permanently satisfy that yearning.

Don't miss this

Only Christ can live up to the "fairytale claim" we're all hunting for. He reminds us in His Word that "YOU ARE COMPLETE IN ME." (Col. 2:10 NASB.) We can face our own hurts, remove our masks, and even take responsibility for our own lives. But ultimately, only God's love can make us truly whole from the inside out.

What are you waiting for? You say that you don't know how to pray? Well, it's really not tough. A sign used to hang on my office wall that may help you. It reads: "When you don't feel like praying, talk to God about it."

So just put down this book and start talking. He's been waiting since the day you were born to begin listening.

"UNFORGIVENESS IS LIKE
DRINKING A POISON AND
EXPECTING SOMEONE ELSE
TO DIE FROM IT."

—UNKNOWN

Chapter 05

THE POISON THAT WILL KILL YOUR DATING LIFE

MAYBE YOU READ ABOUT IT a few years back in the newspaper. A young college woman (let's call her Molly) was driving home from school for a weekend break when her car died on her. Darkness had already fallen, and a gas station was nowhere in sight. So she had no alternative but to stand on the side of the road, trying to flag down help from an anonymous passerby. She started to grab her cell phone to let her parents know she'd be a little late. But not wanting to worry them, Molly thought she would wait to call them until she had things figured out. ⟶ You're probably ahead of me.

Car after car passed her by, seeming not to see her in the darkness by the side of the road. Finally, a truck pulled up, and two friendly men invited her to jump inside. They seemed more than happy to drive Molly to the nearest gas station so she could get some help. The truck sped away, pointing towards the lights of the next distant town.

But that's where our story turns sour. They never made it to the town. Minutes inside the truck, their moods seemed to change. They pulled off the main interstate, headlights now beaming down a deserted road. The young woman felt her stomach go into a knot. She struggled to get words out from the back seat, trying to register her protest.

"Where are we going?" Molly spoke as her voice began to quiver. No real answer came from the front seat, only a sick kind of laughter.

"You'll see," muttered one of the men.

The details of the story are too horrifying to share. In short, the nightmare every woman prays to allude happened on that night. The two guys forced the young college student from their truck, and each man raped her brutally. Laughing with twisted glee after they had completed their actions, they piled back into their truck. They left their victim stranded, hemorrhaging from their perverted pleasures. No doubt, they were sure she would bleed to death that night, lost in the dark, wooded area, never to share her story with anyone else.

But the college woman knew what she had to do. She realized that to stay in the wooded area would seal her death sentence. So with agonizing effort, Molly crawled back towards the main road to summon help. Two hours later, she had painstakingly inched her way back to the edge of the highway. She laid there, lifting her body up to wave whenever she saw headlights coming in her direction. She knew someone would eventually see her and stop to help.

Finally, the headlights slowed down. Blurry in sight, Molly could not see the vehicle. She just knew it was her only ticket to survival. Someone picked her up. Then a voice she had heard before said, "Guess she's stronger than we thought. Let's take her back to the woods and finish her off. We don't want her talking to anyone about our little visit tonight, do we?" ——→ *true story*

The truck gunned its engine and raced off again. An unimaginable horror began to unfold. In sickening irony, the same two perverted men had spotted Molly's lifeless body along the side of the highway. So now they were not only demented, but determined and angry. They wanted to make sure she never saw another sunrise.

Once again, the two animals satisfied themselves. By the time their truck sped away for the second time, Molly had passed out.

Merciful, I think. But the devastation to both her body and her spirit was horrendous.

Hours passed.

Two frantic parents could get no response from their daughter's cell phone.

State troopers were called who found her deserted car along the side of the highway. A desperate search began in the darkness, knowing that they were working against the clock.

Around 4 A.M. Molly's mutilated body was found. Unconscious and narrowly clinging to life, she was rushed to a nearby intensive care unit.

Three days later, our young heroine opened her eyes for the first time in the hospital. She overheard the doctor speaking in hushed tones to her parents in the corner of the room. "Molly's going to need counseling," he explained to them. "She's survived the trauma of the rapes physically, but it will take years for her to be able to recover from the emotional trauma of what those men did to her. I'll send a psychologist in to see her as soon as she's up to talking. Then she'll slowly begin the long road back to emotional wholeness."

Molly shut her eyes again. But this time, she prayed. "I need Your help, Lord," she whispered from her parched lips. Tubes were going in every direction to and from her body. But before falling back asleep, she asked for the help of the Master Physician. He should understand. After all, brutal people beat and hung His body without cause. Five words later, she ended her prayer.

Four days later, a counselor sensitively entered the intensive care room where our Molly was slowly recovering. The doctor struggled for words. She had heard of the brutality of the crime and knew the long road ahead for the girl emotionally.

"<u>They've caught the two men that did this to you</u>," she whispered softly "I know you must hate them. Anyone would. Are you ready to talk about it yet?"

Our heroine, still struggling for strength, spoke slowly. "They've caught the two guys who raped me?"

"Yes," the doctor answered back firmly. "And they'll get the jail time they deserve. But for your own emotional healing, I'd like to help you deal with your feelings towards those two monsters. I know that sounds crazy now. But I promise you; it will be only for your own well-being. Left unchecked, the bitterness and resentment will eat you alive inside."

Molly reached out her hand slowly to the struggling doctor. "I know," she whispered. "You don't have to explain."

"Pardon?" the nervous lady doc responded.

Silence filled the intensive care unit. The beeps of the hospital monitor seemed to echo off the walls. Then our college friend struggled to speak again.

"I...I'm...a Christian," she whispered slowly. "I know...the power...of forgiveness."

The room froze for a minute. The doctor had no words with which to respond. So slowly, the young woman shared her most life-changing decision.

Time stopped for a moment. Sometimes a human choice is so unhuman that all of heaven seems to lean down to listen.

Molly slowly spoke.

"You see," she whispered. "I let those two men rob me of one night in my life. I don't intend to give them another."

Forgiveness? Christ commands it of us in a most uncensored way. Not for the other person's good, but for our own. Why? Because our wise heavenly Dad knows that "Unforgiveness is like drinking a poison and expecting someone else to die from it."

The quote of all quotes ↙

If you're going to be any part of the dating scene, I don't have many guarantees for you. But one thing is absolutely for sure: You'll have disappointments, hurts, and valid reasons to deeply resent people along the journey. It may be the person you date, a third party who interferes, or someone who simply slices you deeply with the pain of

"YOU SEE," SHE WHISPERED. "I LET THOSE TWO MEN ROB ME OF ONE NIGHT IN MY LIFE. I DON'T INTEND TO GIVE THEM ANOTHER."

rejection. Whatever the cause, pain will be the inevitable result. So decide now if you're going to allow yourself to be chained to that person or not. You see, unforgiveness will emotionally lock you to the offender long after he or she has forgotten about the situation.

→ *Sound familar?*

Dating, and even friendship, can fill your life with some pretty raw moments. People can do and say some really stupid, painful things. But fortunately, forgiveness is a (choice) not an (emotion). That's why Jesus could command us to forgive "seventy times seven" in just one day.

He gave us that directive for our own good, not the other person's. So whatever the journey for you, refuse to allow unforgiveness to take root in your heart.

A great book named *The Bible* calls it "being bound to the tormentors." That's a pretty accurate picture of what unforgiveness and resentment will do in your life. So for your own sake, let it go. If not, you will be drinking a relational poison that will slowly destroy not only your dating life, but also your very insides.

Sound tough? Sometimes it is. But once again, it's Christ's uncensored truth.

THERE IS HARDLY ANY
ACTIVITY ON EARTH WHICH
IS STARTED WITH SUCH
TREMENDOUS HOPES AND
YET WHICH FAILS SO
REGULARLY AS LOVE.

—ERICH FROMM

Chapter
06

BREAKING UP WITHOUT FALLING APART

IT ALL HAPPENED MANY YEARS AGO—so many years ago that I can now tell the story. Keep reading. You'll understand. His name was Cody. He was a great guy who was in his early twenties. He started coming to our ministry and chose to give his life to Christ. It was amazing to watch his transformation.

But only a few months into his newfound faith, a romantic interest burst onto the scene. I remember cautioning Cody that he was letting his heart get too attached…too soon. But what did I know?

A few months into the relationship, it became apparent that things were going south. Cody was agonizingly pathetic in his willingness to "do anything to keep her." But much like a starving little dog, the more he groveled, the more unappealing he became to her.

It's a true story I shared in the intro, but bears repeating here.

The handwriting was on the wall, but I just didn't know *what* wall.

Fast forward a few weeks later. The young lady officially broke up with Cody No amount of begging, flowers, or notes could change her mind. It was done…finished…officially over. Cody was deeply depressed. I remember trying to cheer him up. I bought him a Hallmark coffee mug that read, "It's better to have loved and lost…than to be stuck with a loser for the rest of your life." He laughed when I gave the mug to him. But his eyes told me that the whole situation was still no laughing matter. **It gets worse…**

I tried to help him. I promise you I did. But nothing could have prepared me for what happened in the next few weeks. Cody committed a really senseless crime. He was thrown into jail and would have been out in a few weeks—a month at tops. But he never made it out. I got a phone call early one morning from the county jail. They said Cody had listed me as his "next of kin" when they locked him up. The man on the other end of the line stumbled over his words. Finally he blurted out, "Mrs. Mayo, we have some very rough news to tell you. We found Cody this morning in his cell… dead. He hanged himself last night."

Whatever the guy said to me after that point, I don't remember a word of it. My world stood still. Cody had taken his own life largely because he had "broken up and fallen apart." A few hours later, when I arrived to do the final identification of his body, they showed me the note he had penciled on the jail wall to Hailey just before he hung himself—he would "always love her."

How agonizing. How meaningless. What a loss. Cody would have been around 45 now if he had chosen to live. And there would have been another woman in his life...probably children...and a million other meaningful things that would have erased the pain of that shattering season. But the uncensored truth is that there will be no "new season" because he is gone. So let me briefly give you some simple guidelines towards "breaking up without falling apart." Dr. Les Parrott has a great book called *Relationships* which devotes a lengthy chapter to this subject. You might want to pick it up. Let me summarize some of his main suggestions along with some of my own:

SPECIAL THOUGHTS IF YOU ARE THE "HEART BREAKER":

01. **Don't breakup the first time you feel like it.** Emotions come and go. Remember: Love is not an EMOTION, but a CHOICE.

02. If, after time and prayer, you still believe you want to breakup, **have the guts to be honest about it and avoid the temptation to keep putting it off.** None of us enjoy this role. But it's not fair to think that you'll just let the person down "gently" by giving him or her the silent treatment. Have the courage to speak honestly and to tell him or her that you are sincerely sorry, but that it is not working. *Remember that the longer you put it off, the more pain you cause.*

03. **If you're a Christian, avoid the temptation to blame your breakup on the Lord.** (i.e. "I don't want to do this, but the Lord told me in prayer last night that I needed to breakup with you.") Give me a break! I'm not saying that it's wrong to pray about breaking up. But don't make God the "bad guy." Face the hard, cold reality that your feelings have changed and you no longer want to date the other person. *(So put the 'God card' away)*

04. **Make the breakup gentle, but clear and clean.** Maybe begin by telling the other person what you honestly like and appreciate about him or her. Express what you've appreciated about the relationship in general. Share how awkward and tough it is for you to say what you are about to say. But then say it straight out: "I want to breakup." Explain your decision in terms of your

own feelings and values, but don't use this as an opportunity to pinpoint everything you think is wrong about the other person.

05. **Don't make promises that will be really tough to keep.** (i.e. "I want us to remain really close friends.") No fair. If you keep talking to the person, they will receive this as a signal of hope. Have the courage to cut the relationship off cleanly. And when you get lonely a couple of weekends from now, don't cheapen the whole process by calling up the other person to "hang out." At that point, you are a self-centered user. You have a perfect right to breakup. But you *don't* have a right to dangle the other person over an emotional "Hades" while you selfishly meet your own emotional whims.

06. **Keep your mouth shut and stay away.** Guard against the temptation to share private information with others or to make the other person look bad in an effort to justify your breakup. You've already "won" by initiating the breakup. Don't feel you need to take it any further (unless, of course, there has been some form of abusive behavior involved). Then STAY AWAY. The other person will have a really tough time healing if you keep "showing up" everywhere he or she is. Even if the other person continues to fight for personal communication with

you, consistently continue to refuse. Whatever the cost, take the high road on all of this, my friend.

SPECIAL THOUGHTS IF YOU ARE ON THE OTHER END OF THIS PAINFUL BREAKING UP BUSINESS

01. **Face reality. Do yourself a favor by not holding on to false hope.**
The Bible says, "Hope which is postponed makes a person's heart sick." How true. All of us have a tough time coming to terms with rejection. But I beg you to face the reality of the situation. Why? Because the price you pay for denial is often your dignity. When you substitute desperation for dignity, it's never a pretty picture. But, it doesn't have to be that way.

02. **Let yourself feel and cry.** Dr. Les Parrott says, "You ski the black diamond slopes, walk barefoot on hot asphalt, and skydive for fun. So what's a little romantic split? Truth is, a breakup is one of the toughest things you'll ever experience. It's heart wrenching, and you deserve to feel lousy. So give yourself over to the agony and have a good cry. You'll feel better. Scientific studies have shown that tears actually release depression-purging hormones so that you begin to feel better physically and emotionally after a good cry. It literally cleanses your soul. So

Guys, it's ok for you too.

express your sadness rather than keeping it in. The healing will begin all the sooner."[6]

03. **If the depression lasts several months after the breakup, you might need some help from a professional.** That doesn't mean you're weak or psycho. That just means that your hormones have maybe gotten messed up. The same hormonal imbalances that create diabetes in some people can also create significant depression in others. Realize this and go to a doctor for some help. Sustained hormonal depression *does* happen to devoted Christians. Please know this has nothing to do with your walk with Christ. Please just get some help.

> RESENTMENT IS
> **ALLOWING** SOMEONE
> WHO HAS **HURT** YOU
> TO **LIVE** RENT-FREE
> IN YOUR MIND.

04. **Refuse to keep communicating and befriending the other person, as much as you will want to.** Every time you talk or hang out, you're just ripping the scabs off the emotional wounds that are starting to heal. So stay clear of personal contact—at least until you really, really know that you are totally over it. (When the person says, "Can't we still be friends?", your answer needs to be, "No, not until I've had plenty of time to heal and get

over this. So thanks very much, but we need to make this breakup a clean one.")

05. **Steer clear of revenge and bitterness.** Consider re-reading the chapter "The Poison That Will Kill Your Dating Life." Unforgiveness really is like drinking a poison and expecting someone else to die. Here's another one of my favorite "Mayo-isms" on this subject:

Resentment is allowing someone who has hurt you to live rent-free in your mind.

06. **Talk and/or journal to Jesus about your feelings.** Sound strange?  It's really not. That's one of the reasons He is such an amazing God. He really cares about everything that matters to you. In fact, the Bible even says that He is "near to the brokenhearted." Your friends will get tired of hearing you talk about the pain of the situation, but Jesus won't. Journaling to Him about what you're feeling is another really powerful way to start the healing process.

07. **After a few days, stop crying and get busy.** Remember? Right choices will eventually bring right emotions. So start making "right choices"—even when you don't feel like it. Get out

of your house, call up friends, make yourself busy, and *stop rehashing the breakup.* Talking about it over and over only makes it more difficult for you to heal emotionally. I realize that it's tough to turn loose of the memories because they often seem to be your only lifeline to the past. But I beg you. After a few days (or maybe a couple of weeks), for your own good, get busy and get on.

08. **Be careful about quickly dating somebody else on the rebound.** Research even shows that people who begin a relationship on the rebound tend to fall in love with people who will soon reject them. Grasping for another relationship will be especially appealing to you if you used the other person to make you feel good about yourself. Don't cheapen yourself by grabbing at the first human that looks in your direction. You'll regret it.

09. **Remember that as impossible as it feels right now, the sun will really shine again.** In a year from now (or much less in many cases), this heart-ripping person will no longer hold any control over your life. So just know that the dark cloud over your head won't last forever.

In relationships, just like everything else in life, you will have incredible fulfillment if you don't let the painful setbacks put you totally out of the game. Let me remind you that the immortal baseball great, Babe Ruth, struck out 1330 times, a record of failure untouched by any other player in the history of baseball. But nobody ever talks about the strike outs. They only remember that he hit 714 home runs, a record unequalled for 40 years. Someone once asked Babe Ruth the secret of success at the plate. His answer gives us great, uncensored advice for how someone can make it through agonizing breakup seasons: "I just keep goin' up there and keep swingin' at 'em."

So, my long-distance friend, what's my advice to you after a painful breakup? Just make it a clean separation, take some time to heal, and then, "keep swinging!"

"THE WEAKER SEX IS
REALLY THE STRONGER
SEX BECAUSE OF THE
WEAKNESS OF THE
STRONGER SEX FOR THE
WEAKER SEX."

—UNKNOWN

07

WANTED: FEMALE CONTROL FREAKS

OK, GIRLS. It's your big chance. You've heard your whole life that women tend to be control freaks. Bad deal. But now we're talking about an area where Jesus hands out big trophies to you when you control. The area? How far you go romantically in a relationship.

I know what you're thinking. It's a man's responsibility to be in control of this area. I agree, my friend. But if you want to know the honest truth, reality will often throw this area back in the woman's court. Maybe one of the big reasons is because guys are so visual. Most girls are moved by words and emotions. Guys, on the other hand, are turned on by the visual. That basically means that a telephone pole with the right (or wrong) clothes on could make lots of guys have romantic feelings.

It's not just your guy dealing with this

Big deal—read this again.

It all ties together in our uncensored quote: "The weaker sex is often the stronger sex because of the weakness of the stronger sex for the weaker sex." That's a mouthful, wouldn't you say? But take the time to re-read it until you understand what I'm trying to say. The "weaker sex" is obviously the female side of the picture. Please don't get rattled about that. Try glancing at this book's cover, and you'll discover I'm a girl myself. Even more, remember that God designed us girls to be protected by the strength of the men in our lives.

TRUE FREEDOM ISN'T THE RIGHT TO DO WHAT YOU WANT. INSTEAD, IT'S THE POWER TO DO WHAT YOU SHOULD.

Remember the opening story in the Bible about Adam and Eve? Eve (the supposed "weaker sex") influenced Adam to eat from the one tree in the Garden of Eden that was off limits. That's how the whole sin issue started in our world. It's amazing how our human nature always selfishly wants what we aren't supposed to have. Eve could have eaten from any other tree in the Garden. But the enemy convinced her that the one forbidden tree was the one that she really wanted to munch on. (I'm afraid Eve isn't the only person who didn't like to be told "no.")

So what happened? Eve (the supposed "weaker sex") convinced Adam (the supposed "stronger sex") that God the Father was really being a cosmic kill-joy. After all, they needed to be free to eat from any tree in the Garden that they desired. Sound familiar? We still get this whole freedom issue mixed up. You see, true freedom isn't the right to do what you want. Instead, it's the power to do what you should. Adam and Eve didn't get that. But neither do most of us.

The rest of the story is history. Eve convinced Adam to eat from the one forbidden tree, and human nature began the roller coaster of sin. That same cycle has repeated itself through history over and over again. Guys follow a woman's cues (hoping to get what they want) even when the woman's cues are pretty dangerously wrong. Let me say it again: It's *not* supposed to be this way. The men are supposed to be the leaders. (Guys, are you listening?) But truth be told, a woman's influence is pretty dramatic when it comes to issues of romance, intimacy, and self control.

Get it? This chapter is not just for girls

So it's your big chance, ladies. You can be a "control freak" with a positive agenda! Your influence is this strategic arena will make you more attractive to the opposite sex than you might realize. And as for the guys reading this chapter, spend your life trying to be the exception to this principle. After all, who wants to be "just another Adam"?

"WHEN JESUS IS
ALL YOU HAVE,
JESUS WILL BE
ALL YOU NEED."

—CORRIE TEN BOOM
HOLOCAUST SURVIVOR

R-RATED DATING ADVICE FROM THE SCRIPTURES

SONG OF SOLOMON IS A PRETTY "R-RATED" PICTURE of Christ's desire for a close relationship with us. The hormonally driven person will read it and simply think that somebody needed to take a cold shower. But amazingly enough, it's a lot deeper than that. The anthem of the whole book is found in Song of Solomon 6:3: "I am my beloved's and my beloved is mine."

So what am I trying to say? Something really important. Even the one and only God of the Universe "longs to belong"—to somebody, somewhere, sometime. Dr. David Myers, in "The Pursuit of Happiness," publishes some interesting research on the age-old mystery of what makes people happy. Guess what tops the charts. I'll give you some hints. It's not success, money, or even good looks. The clear winner from all the scientific research is relationships—close ones.

Let me blow your mind with another fact. Two independent studies, one done at the University of California and the other at the University of Michigan, found that adults who do not cultivate close personal relationships have premature death rates twice as high as people with frequent personal contact with others.[4] Wow! Move over high cholesterol and lack of exercise. Just give me some friends!

So whether we admit it or not, the uncensored truth is that we all "long to belong." Hollywood knows that's our bottom line. You can't find many blockbusters that don't have romance woven into the plot. Then try listening to music for a while. Sure, styles of music change almost daily, but the repeating theme of our longing for relationship doesn't.

www.readthis.com.

There's only one problem with this whole deal. We have a really warped perspective of relationships. We inwardly think that when we get the right friend (the right "soul mate"), we'll be happy. We spend hours on MySpace trying to cultivate those friendships. We even do pretty scary things like trying to fall in love over the Internet. (Sorry if that's you. But you've got to admit, it's a pretty unrealistic proposition. I call it "Using a *mouse* to find a *spouse!*"

The guys from centuries ago struggled with this same need to belong to someone. But though their language is a little outdated, their wisdom is not. Saint Augustine said powerfully, "My heart is restless, O God, until it rests in Thee." Augustine talked about an invisible but real spot inside all of us. We'll call it our "God Block." That's why no matter how many friends we have, how much money we make, or how perfect our measurements are, we stay inwardly dissatisfied until we have prioritized our relationship with Christ.

if only very-realized this

So what am I suggesting? Don't worry. I'm not asking you to "date God." (It'd be pretty tricky trying to pull that off anyway). I'm just suggesting that you be really, really aware that your internal "longing for belonging" is a driving force we all deal with. Don't pretend it's not there. Just channel it. And in that process, realize that relationship with Jesus Christ is the only place you will find the stability, intimacy, and consistency that can make your heart safe, fulfilled, and whole. That's why I often say something like this to the Lord: "Jesus, I really need You to finish my sentences now. So I come by faith into Your presence, asking You to once again be my best Friend and closest

Confidant. I need to deeply and completely belong to Someone. So once again, Lord, I choose to make that someone You."

What do you do after that? Let me give you a few things that have worked for me:

01. **As I said earlier, when you don't feel like praying, talk to God about it!** (No joke intended. We just sometimes make prayer way too tough.)

02. **When you pray, talk feelings to Him.** In other words, ditch all the "Thee's" and "Thou's" and talk to Jesus about what is really going on inside of you. Talk to Him like the great Dad He really is.

03. **Consider journaling some of your thoughts or prayers.** Don't make this too tough. Just occasionally record some of your prayers or thoughts on paper. I love to write down a Scripture or two that stands out to me. Want to hear this morning's? It comes from Psalm 73:26 where David shows us what he did with his "longing for belonging." It says, "My flesh and my heart may fail, but God is the strength of my heart" (NIV).

Journaling is just for girls. I know lots of sharp guys who journal.

04. **Do something a little out-of-the-box with God.** I mean, all great relationships get stale if you stay in a rut. So occasionally, add

freshness to your relationship by taking a walk while you talk with Him, grabbing some java and journaling at a cool coffee shop, or any other simple way to get out of a rut.

05. **Take the "Longing for Belonging Quiz" on the next page.** Then take a few minutes to evaluate what might need to change in your life to make you a more whole, secure, and complete person.

Happy quiz-taking! I promise you there are no grades at the end of this one.

A+++
just for reading this!

WE ALL HAVE A
"LONGING
FOR
BELONGING."

—DR. LES PARROTT

LONGING FOR BELONGING/QUIZ⁵

TAKE A COUPLE OF MINUTES to give yourself this quiz. Go with your first instinct. Then add up the numbers and see where you're at in all of this. Come on. Be truthful. Nobody's going to see this page but you.

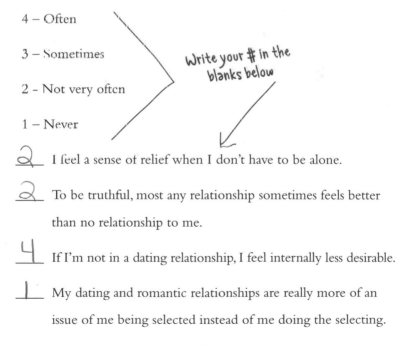

4 – Often

3 – Sometimes

2 - Not very often

1 – Never

Write your # in the blanks below

2 I feel a sense of relief when I don't have to be alone.

2 To be truthful, most any relationship sometimes feels better than no relationship to me.

4 If I'm not in a dating relationship, I feel internally less desirable.

1 My dating and romantic relationships are really more of an issue of me being selected instead of me doing the selecting.

_2_ If I'm honest with myself, I don't have a really clear picture of the personal qualities I look for in a person to date or even be close friends with.

> **EVEN THE ONE AND ONLY GOD OF THE UNIVERSE "LONGS TO BELONG"—TO SOMEBODY, SOMEWHERE, SOMETIME.**

_2_ I don't like to be alone.

_3_ I feel a little bit of panic when I think of not having someone to be close to.

_3_ When I'm dating someone, I feel better about myself.

_3_ My idea of a rotten weekend is not having anyone to hang out with.

_2_ I'm tempted to settle for most any relationship because I don't really know if I can find someone better.

_24_ | TOTAL LONGING FOR BELONGING SCORE

There is a possible total of 40 points in our little quiz. Let me help you interpret your score:

40–30 Thanks for being honest. A score in this range lets you know that this whole area is something you really want to work on. Go back and re-read this chapter and think about actually doing the

4 steps I suggest at the end. You will be so much more secure and happy when you gradually get stronger in the arena of making Jesus the central relationship of your life. (For real. Not just in religious words.) This "longing for belonging" arena is a big deal. So please don't coast here. Get to work! *What are you waiting for?*
Flip back to the beginning of this chapter!

29-20 You're one of those amazing "middle of the road" people. In all honesty, you're not doing bad in this area. But you still have quite a bit of work to do. If you keep drifting in your current direction, your relational world may become pretty disappointing. So do something to get yourself off the fence. (Those 4 questions at the end of the last chapter might be a good starting point for you.) If you're tempted to keep hanging around the center, just remember that the only thing that you ever find in the middle of the road is something that's DEAD!

19-10 Way to go! No, you haven't arrived. But if you had a score in this range, you're making some good progress towards being a secure, whole person internally yourself. I sure hope that security pivots around Jesus.

(Special note to the "19" and "18" point people: Good job, but don't be too overjoyed. Your number was probably higher than your own personal security. So pat yourself on the back and then go back to my suggested 4 points.)

FROM THE LADIES TO THE GUYS:

"WE WANT TO FEEL LIKE YOUR PRINCESS, NOT YOUR CALL GIRL. SO WHEN WE DATE, WORK HARD TO MAKE SURE WE DON'T BECOME YOUR PERSONAL MEAT MARKET. IF YOU GO SLOW ON THE PHYSICAL, YOU'LL SET YOURSELF APART FROM 99% OF THE KNOWN UNIVERSE...AND WE'LL BE CRAZY ABOUT YOU."

Chapter 09

10 THINGS GIRLS WISH GUYS KNEW ABOUT DATING

Note to the male species: Please read!

01. **Guys often seem to use the emotional to get the physical.** That's called being a jerk! Don't do it.

02. **Prioritize communication over romance.** As a matter of fact, to a woman, communication *(is)* romance! So work hard at putting effort into the communication front. After we've dated you for a while, you tell us you can't think of anything to say. That always confuses us because you could think of plenty to say when you were first trying to catch us. Bottom line: We think you stop being a good communicator because you let yourself get lazy and allow too much focus to go on the romantic side of our relationship.

03. **We want to be your girlfriend, not your mother.** Girls are wired to want to follow and look up to the significant guy in their

life. But we can't play mental "pretend games." So though we know you can't be perfect, please try to make the character choices that will give us someone we can honestly respect.)

We want you to be the leader and initiator too. That means even thinking ahead about what we're going to do on dates. Don't just pick us up and say, "What do you want to do tonight?" Even strong girls want to feel like they are dating a guy who is a leader and someone they can quietly lean on.

04. **Tell us often what you appreciate about us, and don't focus primarily on our appearance.** We want honest affirmation and thrive when you give it to us. But try to focus more on complimenting our "insides" than our "outsides." Yes, we want you to think that we're hot and good-looking. But we gain mountains of security when we feel like your commitment to us is more about *who we are* than about *how we look.*

05. **Don't be a "player."** Guard and protect our hearts. If things are not going anywhere in our dating relationship (or if your feelings change), please don't drag things out. Have the guts to speak privately and honestly to us. All along the journey, please be clear about your intentions and refuse to play emotional

this is so HUGE!

games with us to get what you want physically or to build your ego up.

It's a fact of life: Girls' hearts get tied up and involved way faster than guys' hearts seem to. So please don't send signals in private to us that you don't really mean (i.e. using romantic voice tones, words, or glances). To you, those signals may be no big deal. But to a girl, those little things send loud messages. So please don't say or hint things unless you really mean them. (We're sick of hearing you say, "I don't understand how she could have gotten that idea!")

06. **Remember that what we feel is as real to us as what you think.** So listen deeply when we talk. And "don't try to fix it till you feel it."

07. **Be strong enough to be weak sometimes.** Be "steel wrapped in velvet." Strong guys are able to easily admit when they are wrong, ask forgiveness, and seek advice from others. Sometimes your tough, macho front is a turn-off to us. Be man enough to be vulnerable and truthful. You see, as guys, you will lead us through your strengths; but we will connect to you through your weaknesses. You go up in our eyes when you are man enough to ask for forgiveness or help. *Way, way up*

08. **We don't want to feel like your personal meat-market.** So go slow on the physical and you'll set yourself apart from 99% of everyone else we've ever dated. If you control your sexual desires and what you say to us, you will be the guy that every girl is looking for. You may think that strength is benching 250 pounds. But we think strength is having your character be more powerful than your hormones.

When you don't try to go too far with us, we read it as a signal of respect and value. You make us feel like your "princess" instead of your "call girl," and we become even more attracted to you because we see you as a man of self-control. Remember: Pushing us to go too far with you isn't love to us at all. It makes us feel like you care more about satisfying your own sexual desires than taking care of us. *and our respect level drops way off*

We may even give in to you romantically. (Remember? Guys use the emotional to get the physical. And girls use the physical to get the emotional.) But if we do give in to you, we'll usually feel guilty the next day and become emotionally clingy and/or demanding. So stop the cycle before it starts. If you do, you'll be the guy every girl wants to belong to.

09. **Don't spend big bucks on gifts for us or on our dates.** We treasure simple things that you put time and emotional energy into. So congratulations! You don't need to send us a dozen yellow roses very often. We will be just as happy with a daisy you bring to our front door one night with a sweet little note. As far as places we go while we're dating, occasionally let us dress up and take us somewhere really nice. But most of the time, we are really impressed with low-cost dates that you took time to plan and put effort into.

So congratulations! You don't need a big budget to date us successfully. You just need a big heart.

10. **Nothing is more attractive to us than a man of God full of character, guts, and integrity.** Again, we don't expect you to be perfect, but we really want to be able to look up to you. So fight to be more than "just another one of the guys." We're not asking you to be Billy Graham, but we are asking you to be authentic in your pursuit after God. Despite what the "women's libbers" say, we really do want you to be the leader. This is especially true in the spiritual arena. So know that your authentic pursuit after God only makes us want to pursue you more.

Secret:
Godliness holds an incredible attraction to us

SPECIAL NOTE FROM THE GUYS TO LADIES:

IF WHAT YOU'RE SHOWING
ISN'T ON THE MENU,
KEEP IT COVERED.

—JUSTIN LOOKADOO

Chapter

10

Girls—
Read this

↓ ↙

12 THINGS GUYS WISH GIRLS KNEW ABOUT DATING

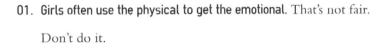

01. **Girls often use the physical to get the emotional.** That's not fair. Don't do it.

02. **Appreciate a guy's battle against lust.** Help us out instead of "dangling us over a cliff"! We're turned on easily by the visual. So if you want us to treat you like a lady, you need to carry yourself like one. (i.e. Don't "paint" your clothes on and then wonder why we tried to push things too far.)

We want to be guys of integrity in the romantic realm, but we need your help. We know as guys that we are supposed to be the leaders and draw the right lines romantically. But sometimes it's just really tough. So help us out by making your standards clear and then remaining true to those standards, even if we turn our brains off when things get hot. In other

73

words, don't happily "jump off the mountain" with us and then wonder why we have a tough time stopping the free-fall in mid-air.

03. **The less you date, the more attractive you are to the right guys.** Don't let yourself become "easy" or "cheap" just because you're lonely. We want the secret impression that you could date often if you *wanted* to, but that you are too selective to go out with "just anybody."

04. **At all costs, avoid the drama.** We get enough of that at the movies. We don't want to data a "drama queen." Enough said.

05. **Let me feel like I'm chasing and pursuing you in the relationship instead of you being the initiator.** There are times when we guys appreciate the confidence that a little bit of chasing from your end brings. But most of the time, let us feel like we're coming after you. (Just so you know, guys often view girls who come on strong as easy or desperate.)

While we're on this point, go easy on the phone calls. We know that girls call guys these days. But let us initiate most of the calling from our end. If we don't call you very often, face the painful truth that we're probably not as interested in you as you are in us.

06. **Hear what I mean when I talk to you, not always what I say.** Don't attach more meaning to my words than I really mean to give them. Guys and girls communicate on different levels.

Let me explain. When we guys say, "I've never felt like this about a girl before," we really mean, "I didn't feel these exact same feelings with the last girl I dated." The normal female species, though, hears us as saying, "I'm crazy about you. We are probably soul-mates because I've never met anyone in the world like you before. So go buy a wedding magazine and start making bridal plans."

GUYS USE THE EMOTIONAL TO GET THE PHYSICAL; AND GIRLS USE THE PHYSICAL TO GET THE EMOTIONAL.

Big Deal

Let's take another one. When a guy says, "I love you," he's using the same words he would use to talk to his mom or describe how he feels about football. But a girl hears those words to mean, "You are my one and only. You are the queen of my life, and I want to collect Social Security together."

Do guys lie? Not exactly. A guy is just interested in conquest. He's often unconsciously trying to find the right combination of words to help him advance in the game. So when a guy says some of these things, he really does mean what he's saying— just not with the same intensity as a girl often takes it. We guys aren't trying to lie to you or purposefully mislead you. We just have a different perspective about the words we're telling you.

Remember: Guys use the emotional to get the physical; and girls use the physical to get the emotional.

07. **If what you're showing isn't on the menu, keep it covered!** (Re-read slowly if you're confused. If you're still confused, go ask your grandmother what we're trying to say.)

08. **Be mysterious sometimes; and be fun lots of the time.** What do we mean by "mysterious"? We just don't want you to tell us all your deepest secrets during the first month we go out. We want to feel like you really care about us but that we haven't totally conquered you in the first few months of our relationship. Go study that weird grin on the Mona Lisa and

occasionally use it with us. It keeps us wanting to know you better rather than feeling like you're "easy" and pretty cheap. We complain about "never understanding women." But if you want to know the truth, that mystery is pretty appealing to us.

As far as the "fun" thing goes, laugh *with* us, not *at* us. We know we can be pretty corny, but our egos really feel great if you find us funny sometimes. Girls that are fun to hang around are also really attractive.

Maybe you don't like the same sports we do. But try to fake it till you make it! In other words, be interested in some of the fun things that are a big deal in a man's world. It will make you the envy of all the other guys in the known universe.

REMEMBER: AS YOUR **DEPENDENCY** GROWS, OUR **RELATIONSHIP** GOES!

09. **Let me be the leader, but express your opinions and don't let me make all the decisions.** Yeah, yeah…I know I'm supposed to figure out what we're doing on most of our dates. But help me out occasionally. This can get pretty tough. I don't want to date a "yes darling" machine. I want to date a girl with her own

style and personality. So get your mouth open and voice your opinions. You don't want to be viewed as a cheap "romance robot." So plug your brain in and give me a run for my money.

10. **Don't smother me by acting like you want to be with me 24/7.** And

Remember: sometimes less is more

try not to come across as (emotionally needy) or like a control freak. Strong guys run from girls who are clingy or possessive. We eventually feel caged in, trapped, or smothered. So give us air. Let us spend time with our guy friends; and make sure you spend time with your girlfriends. Make us secretly plot because we want *more* time with you, not because we're trying to cut the invisible umbilical cord you've tied to us.

Remember: As your dependency GROWS, our relationship GOES!

11. **Guys need modesty from girls they date, even though (inside their animal brains) they don't always act like they want it.** *Are you always going to give a guy what he (wants,) or will you be woman enough to occasionally give him what he really (needs?)* Your answer to that question will determine if you are mature enough to date—whether you're 16 or 26.

12. **Find your security in Christ, not in us.** Granted, when we first start dating, it might be flattering that you act like we are the

epicenter of your personal universe. But over time, this kind of insecurity becomes less and less attractive, and more and more a turn off.

Remember that you are most attractive when you are a woman of integrity. We're not looking for "Mother Theresa" or anything (Thank God!), but we are looking for a girl who makes her relationship with Jesus Christ her primary security, not us. After all, it makes us nervous when you pressure us to be "god" in your life. That job looks a little out of our league. So let Jesus handle that responsibility, not us.

NEVER BECOME SO PREOCCUPIED WITH WHO YOU WANT THAT YOU FORGET TO BE WHO YOU ARE.

HOW TO HAVE MORE FRIENDS THAN YOU'LL EVER DESERVE

A GUARANTEED WAY TO PREDICT YOUR FUTURE

DO YOUR FRIENDS HAVE FLEAS?

Don't try and use this this crystal ball!

You'll have to read this chapter to find the answer

12 THINGS GUYS WISH GIRLS KNEW

THE VOICE
YOU CAN'T IGNORE

FRIENDSHIPS

14
THINGS
GIRLS
WISH GUYS
KNEW

THE BIG
SECRET
OF
MAKING FRIENDS

"THE DAY WILL COME WHEN, AFTER HARNESSING THE WINDS, THE TIDES AND GRAVITATION, WE SHALL HARNESS FOR GOD THE ENERGIES OF LOVE. AND ON THAT DAY, FOR THE SECOND TIME IN THE HISTORY OF THE WORLD, MAN WILL HAVE DISCOVERED FIRE."

—TEILHARD DE CHARDIN

11

HOW TO HAVE MORE FRIENDS THAN YOU'LL EVER DESERVE

(It was a night I will never forget.) One of those bittersweet evenings that

etches its way forever into your heart. You see, I had been the leader

of a youth ministry called Cross Current. My husband was the senior

pastor of the church, and we had arrived in Rockford, Illinois, to

pastor there almost thirteen years before this concluding evening. The

youth church that I had lovingly grown from around 50 students

to nearly 1,000 students each week was hosting a farewell for me

that night. My husband and I were going to be moving on to take

another ministry position in a different state. The night was awesome

and unforgettable. People flew in from all over the nation and then

lovingly shared their appreciation for me. I laughed as much as I

cried. The theme of the evening was "A Legacy of No Regrets."

Through the thirteen-year run in Rockford, I had followed a simple pattern every week at the conclusion of our youth church service. I wouldn't leave the amphitheater until the last teenager or young adult who wanted to talk with me had been given the opportunity. My philosophy was simple: "If you're willing to wait, I'm *Why?* *Because real* willing to stay!" So on this farewell evening, my pattern of lingering *ministry is* *about taking care* to talk remained the same. *of people*

For obvious reasons, the line was really long that night. If my memory serves me correctly, I finished talking to the last person at about 4 A.M. People left, ate dinner, came back, and fell asleep among the seats as they waited.

Around 2 A.M., a sad, lonely looking young woman became my conversational companion. I knew her only vaguely. But it was obvious from the beginning of the conversation that she had stayed to discuss something very important to her that night. She fumbled for words. Finally, she just blurted out, "Look at all these people who are still here, waiting to talk to you. Look at what time it is! What did you do to have this many friends?"

Her words came with such emotion that they abruptly jolted me out of my tiredness. I wanted to just give a simple answer and then hug her farewell. But the Jesus inside of me was not OK with that approach. My mind raced back to my closing message I had shared with Cross Current the week before. Its title? "The Mantle of Love." On a small gift I created for everyone present that night, I had printed the quote I shared with you at the beginning of this chapter:

"Someday, after we have mastered the winds and waves, the tides and gravity, we will harness the energy and power of God's love. And then, for the second time in the history of mankind, the world will have discovered fire."

As my sincere young friend sat there staring at me, waiting for my "magic formula," I knew my answer was going to be simpler than she was expecting.

"I...I assign top priority to my relationships," I said.

She stared back blankly at me. (In her head, she was probably thinking, "I waited till two in the morning to hear *that* answer!")

The silence was a little uncomfortable for me. So I simply repeated my seven-word answer to her again. "I assign top priority to my relationships." Nothing too profound. It was just the bottom line for me.

I went on to share with her: "I've watched people who are deeply loved. After their relationship with Jesus Christ, I've noticed that they make other people a high priority in their lives. So through the past thirteen years of ministry here, I've always tried to remember that the people are ultimately more important than the pulpit."

I paused, but her eyes seemed to beg me to continue. "Everybody is really busy. But I've just developed a lifestyle that prioritizes building significant relationships in my life. They don't start out as significant. But as I have consistently invested in individual people, they have become priceless to me."

Her eyes darted around the room again. The sight of slumped bodies still waiting to talk to me seemed to add fresh passion to her question. "But what about all these people here tonight? You couldn't have hung out with all of them! Why are they still here?"

"Beats me!" I laughingly agreed. "You're sure right that most of these people haven't had deep friendships with me. But in the brief exchanges I've had with many of them, I tried to make them feel like they were the only person in my world at that moment. It's the old expression you've probably heard, 'Wherever you are, be all the way there.' I guess it just boils down to treating other people the way I would want to be treated myself." /// — It really is that SIMPLE!

Her faced softened. Something seemed to click inside for her.

"So you get all of this by prioritizing people in your life?"

A yawn slipped from her face as she finished the question. She tried to hide it, but we both knowingly smiled. She glanced over her shoulder at the next person stretched out near the platform, waiting for his "turn at bat."

"Just remember, my friend," I concluded with her, "the Bible says that 'where your treasure is, your heart will be also.' In Cross Current, I sometimes said that 'Treasure = T³.' It's a Mayoism for 'time, thoughts, and talk.' So wherever you place your time, thoughts, and talk, you'll eventually find to be your treasure. I can't promise that you'll one day have friends crazy enough to wait up this late to talk with you. But I *can* promise you that if you place consistent energy into the unselfish cultivation of relationships, you'll be a happy person."

She leaned towards me, as though signaling the end of the conversation and her desire for one last hug.

The hug was good and meaningful. She seemed so painfully lonely that I wanted to take special care of her.

"One last thing," she said as she stood to leave. "Could I see the platinum ring they gave you tonight?"

Lovingly, I slipped the ring off my finger that had been presented to me earlier that evening. I handed it to her. She read aloud the engraving placed on the inside of it.

"'A legacy of no regrets,'" she spoke slowly. "Maybe one day, people will be able to say that about me.'"

IF YOU WANT
TO HAVE FRIENDS,
BE YOUR OWN
FRIEND FIRST.

12

THE VOICE YOU CAN'T IGNORE

The date was February 12, 1976. A strange but significant announce-
ment was made public. For the first time, the world was told the
contents of Abraham Lincoln's pockets on the night he was assassinated.
So what's the big deal? Believe me. At the risk of sounding cheesy,
Abe Lincoln still speaks to us from his pockets. Inside the famous
President's pockets were two pairs of glasses, an ivory pocketknife, and
a large white Irish linen handkerchief, slightly used, with "A. Lincoln"
embroidered in red. But one other significant thing was found carefully
tucked in his pocket that night. It was a newspaper article on his presi-
dency written by a guy named John Bright. The article had obviously
been carefully cut and folded, as though Lincoln had taken precise
measures to make sure he would be able to refer to it often.

So what's so unusual about that article? First, you need to know something about the political tenor at that time to understand. During the period surrounding Lincoln's assassination, the press had become relentlessly negative and brutal on the President and his leadership. Newspaper after newspaper talked about the poor job he was doing, his lack of leadership skill, and the negative impact of his administration. But, oddly enough, Lincoln was smart enough not to keep any of *those* newspaper articles in his pockets for frequent review. The article by John Bright was one of the few highly favorable newspaper articles published about Lincoln during this entire time period. Yet, wisely enough, this one was the only article Lincoln chose to keep close to him. I bet when things got tough, he pulled it out of his pocket and secretly glanced at the positive words again.

So let me ask you an important question: What kind of newspaper articles are you carrying in the pockets of your mind? Christian counselors call this "self-talk." The term references the number of words that float through our unconscious minds constantly. Consider the facts. Approximately 70 percent of our waking day is spent in one or more kinds of communication. You speak out loud at a rate of 150–200 words per minute. But research tells us that you talk privately to yourself ("self talk") at approximately 1,300 words per

minute. Big difference, wouldn't you say?

At any given moment, we are saying things to ourselves in

rapid-fire succession. That constant undercur-

Big difference + big deal

rent of self-talk affects every area of our lives—

our emotions, our energy, our

YOU SPEAK OUT LOUD AT A RATE OF 150–200 WORDS PER MINUTE. YOU TALK PRIVATELY TO YOURSELF ("SELF TALK") AT APPROXIMATELY 1,300 WORDS PER MINUTE.

mood, our self-confidence, and

definitely our relationships. That's

why the Scripture says so clearly,

"As [a man] thinks in his heart, so

is he" (Prov. 23:7 AMP). That's also

why we ultimately can't treat other

people any better than we inwardly

treat ourselves.

Garbage in— garbage out

Abe Lincoln knew the importance of feeding your own mind with

positive encouragement rather than rehearsing over and over again all

the negatives. How are you doing with that one? It's a matter of life

or death, you know.

Let me tell you a supposedly true story that illustrates this life-giving

power of self-talk. A man was traveling across the country by sneaking

rides on freight trains. On one particular night, he climbed into what he thought was just another boxcar and shut the door. The train jolted right after this, clamping the door firmly shut. Only seconds later, the man noticed how cold the boxcar was. I'm sure he yelled for help. But apparently, no one heard him. His panic was easy to understand. He'd found himself *locked inside a refrigeration boxcar!*

The guy had to deal with some pretty loud self-talk that night. Sure that he would soon freeze to death, he began to scratch a message on the floor of the car to his family. But the guy never finished the message. Sometime the next day, a repairman from the railroad opened the door of the refrigeration boxcar and found the man dead. He appeared to have frozen to death, motionless on the floor, while attempting to write a farewell message.

For real!

But want to hear the weird ending? The repairman had come to *fix* the refrigeration on the boxcar. (It turns out that the temperature inside the car never went below fifty degrees during the night—not nearly cold enough to kill the man.) So the obvious question begs to be answered: Why did the guy die?

The answer can be explained only one way: He *told himself* he was freezing to death!

So the question now comes to you, my friend. Whose internal self-talk is yours most like—Abe Lincoln's or our frozen friend? What are you telling yourself about yourself? It's a life-changing question when we talk about cultivating great friendships. In truth, your own voice is the one voice you can't ignore.

Remember: The most important friendship you will ever cultivate will be with yourself.

The choice is always our

REMEMBER: THE MOST IMPORTANT FRIENDSHIP YOU WILL EVER CULTIVATE WILL BE WITH YOURSELF.

"SHOW ME YOUR FRIENDS, AND I'LL SHOW YOU YOUR FUTURE."

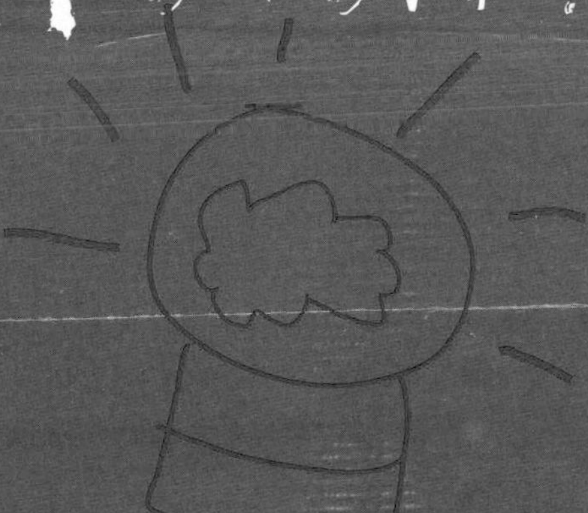

A GUARANTEED WAY TO PREDICT YOUR FUTURE

Everybody wants to know what's ahead in their life. So let's experiment with a few questions for fun: What kind of person will you marry? What kind of reputation will you build for yourself? How fulfilled and successful will you be in your career? Take the questions out as far into your future as you want. You can even predict several parts of your own funeral with accuracy!

There are a million big questions about the future. But how do you get answers? After all, crystal balls aren't exactly on God's "Top Ten" list for guidance. So what is?

Proverbs hints at the answer when it says, "Don't hang out with angry people; don't keep company with hotheads. Bad temper is contagious. So don't get infected" (Prov. 22:24 MSG). Did you catch that? It says that we "catch" the personality of the people we spend much time with.

So if you want to predict what kind of person you will be like in the future, all you have to do is check out the friendship circle you have created in your present. This biblical principle proves true of all character traits—not just anger. Character is contagious! Let me reword this principle for you. I often say, "Show me your friends, and I'll show you your future."

I can just hear you now. "Come on, Jeanne. Isn't that pretty overstated?"

I don't think so. And my experience for nearly four decades of working with teenagers, university students, and people in general has made me even more a believer. If I get to know the kind of people that someone surrounds himself with, I've got a pretty accurate glimpse of his own insides (or where his insides are heading). Let those relationships continue, and they become a great predictor of the person's future—at almost every level.

I want this principle to be wrong. Please believe that. I've lost count of the number of great people who have gone on some major spiritual tale-spins because they thought they were "the exceptions." Yet friendships predict a person's future with almost agonizing accuracy. It doesn't happen the first time a couple of people hang out together… or the second. But before long, attitudes start to change. Goals start to change. Conversations start to change. And with the passing of just a little time, the person's inner-self and relationship with Christ (or lack of it) start to change too.

Ever wonder… How did this happen?

Now don't get me wrong. This principle works positively just as consistently as it works negatively. Start hanging around positive, Christ-honoring people, and you will slowly find those values rubbing off on you too. This principle even applies to more areas than just the spiritual arena. So take heart! If you begin to spend time with people who value hard work and decent grades, you're on your way towards making Einstein proud of you.

Just a couple of days ago, I tried to communicate this principle to a sharp senior in high school. He had hit a pretty bumpy point in his walk with Christ. He dropped by my office for some feedback. Listen in to our conversation:

Jeanne: "Matt, do me a favor. Stand on this chair for a minute."

Matt: "The chair? You want me to stand on this chair? Any special reason?"

Jeanne: "Work with me, friend. This conversation is going some-where. I promise."

Matt: "OK…whatever floats your boat" (mumbled as he reluctantly climbed on top of a nearby chair).

Jeanne: "Now, grab my hand and pull me up…up to your level."

Matt: "I still don't get it, but give me your hand anyway" (said with a macho grin because of his football frame). ⟶

Sound effects from "Muscular Matt": Grunt…grunt. Pull…pull.

IN THE RELATIONAL WORLD, IT WILL ALWAYS BE EASIER TO PULL PEOPLE DOWN THAN TO PULL PEOPLE UP.

End result: Weak, female Jeanne is still left planted firmly on the floor with very little effort.

Jeanne: "So that 'pulling me up jazz' didn't work so well, did it? Let's see how another approach works."

Next action: Weak, non-weight-lifting Jeanne gives one significant yank to the arm of "Mighty Matt" (the macho but now humbled football player).

End result: Matt is pulled down easily from his position on top of the chair. Still a little confused, he regains his balance and then speaks.

Matt: "OK…OK. What am I supposed to learn from that?"

Jeanne: "Something very simple but also very important. In the relational world, it will always be easier to pull people down than to pull people up. That's why Jesus is so serious about the people who make up your close friendship circle."

Matt: (Heavy sigh…knowing look) "I hear you. I know what you're trying to say to me."

Jeanne: "You're a smart guy, my friend. The next move is up to you."

Matt: (Long pause. Looking at feet. Quiet response.) "Maybe my friends *do* have something to do with the mess I'm in right now. I probably need to do some thinking."

Matt had a decision. Truth could be cheaply discarded or lived by. Time will tell his decision, just like it will yours.

Your name is probably not Matt, but the principle works the same for all of us. That's why the Bible says, "Spiritual light should not have heart-to-heart companionship with spiritual darkness." (Eph. 5:8–11

AMP, author's paraphrase.) Rationalize all you want, but it's a biblical law that comes through as consistently as gravity.

So want to predict your future with amazing accuracy? Study closely the three friends you spend the most time with. Study their attitudes, their priorities, their discipline, their values—the whole package. Then step back and realize that unless you change your friendship circle, that's exactly where you're heading.

Heart-to heart companionship

What's that? You say that you're "pulling them up" spiritually?

Sorry. It just doesn't work that way. Go find a chair of your own to stand on. No matter how great your intentions, it's always easier to "pull down" than to "pull up." Who needs a crystal ball when future predictions are this simple?

It's God's uncensored truth: Show me your friends and I'll show you your future.

"WE MAKE A **LIVING** BY WHAT WE **GET.** WE MAKE A **LIFE** BY WHAT WE **GIVE.**"

—SIR WINSTON CHURCHILL

Chapter

14

THE BIG SECRET OF MAKING FRIENDS

I promise you that I don't deserve all the great friends I have. That's not fake modesty. It's just reality. But I can also promise you that I can identify one of the simple reasons why I have so many amazing friends. Are you ready? It's going to sound so simple that you'll want to write off my answer. But please don't.

I've taught myself to be an authentically affirming, encouraging person to everyone I'm privileged to connect with under every possible circumstance.

Sounds simple, but it really isn't. You see, I didn't grow up in a home that majored on the positives. My mom loved me fiercely and did everything in her power to take care of me. My dad, though, had a pretty serious alcohol problem. So in public, he treated me like "his little princess." But in the privacy of our home, my dad's drinking and anger problem created a very different reality. I remember one night when he asked me to give a brief piano recital for one of his drinking friends. Apparently, my efforts were not up to his standards. So the recital ended abruptly when he closed the piano lid on my fingers, mumbling something about my needing to practice more.

I was only 8 – Not fun.

Early in my teenage years, I sized up the situation. I could either get "bitter" or "better." The second option had much more appeal. So I began to mentally study people who seemed secure, well liked, and fulfilled in their Christianity. Repeatedly, I noticed that the people who were the most loved themselves gave the most love away. The people who seemed to have the most affirmation coming in their direction always seemed to be those who gave away sincere affirmation first. Thus, the people who had the most friends always seemed to be the people who prioritized first affirming and encouraging *their* friends.

Oh, granted, there were the obvious exceptions. I saw the popular football player or gorgeous cheerleader who didn't seem to fit the pattern. They were self-centered and found their friendships in their looks, abilities, or circumstances. But looking ahead a few years, it didn't take a counseling degree to figure out that their friendships were as short-lived as the particular circumstances that created them.

I decided to build my life around a biblical principle that seemed to work for everyone for as long as they sincerely functioned in that truth. That's when I began to teach myself to purposefully look for things in other people that I could sincerely appreciate—and then verbalize it to them.

We live in a really sarcastic world. Sarcasm is king in so many youth and young adult circles, especially when it causes other people to laugh. But I have a tough time picturing Jesus taking part in that kind of relationship building. I think He more majored around truth and authentic affirmation. Over and over, the New Testament makes it clear that He looked past the worst in people and took time to call out the very best in them. That's why He looked at a big-mouthed guy named "Simon" and changed his life when He befriended him.

You'll have to practice this.

"Simon" means "little pebble" in the Greek language. But Jesus said, "Buddy, I honestly see some great things inside of you. So I'm going to focus on the positive things in your life so I can help you grow. As a matter of fact, I'm going to change your name from 'Simon' ('little pebble') to 'Peter' ('big boulder')." Now granted, Peter wasn't exactly a "big boulder" for the entirety of his friendship with Jesus. But because Christ repeatedly reinforced the positive in Peter's life, Jesus gradually transformed Peter into the leader of the New Testament Church.

Have you ever heard of Dale Carnegie's classic old leadership book called *How to Win Friends and Influence People?* Before you start laughing under your breath, let me tell you that it stayed on the *New York Times* bestseller list for 10 years, a record that hasn't been matched since. After selling more than 10 million copies, the book continues to sell at the rate of 200,000 a year.

MAKE SURE YOU GIVE AWAY AUTHENTIC AFFIRMATION AND ENCOURAGEMENT. AND DO IT OFTEN.

OK, let me give you the bottom-line secret that made Carnegie a legend. It's contained in his chapter, "The Big Secret of Dealing with People." The "big secret" really wasn't an original idea to him, though. Christ transformed twelve pretty rough guys into disciples by prioritizing it. The best managers, coaches, and teachers use this simple "secret" every day of their lives. As a matter of fact, when you've been at your best with your friends and other people, you've used this "secret" too. Are you ready for Carnegie's life-changing friendship key?

"Be hearty in your approbation and lavish in your praise."

Now let me translate that into understandable English for you: "Be sure you deeply appreciate people and sincerely communicate lots of authentic encouragement to them."

That's it. That's the big revelation that made Carnegie's book the most repeated one on the *New York Times* bestseller list in all of modern-day history. His life-changing secret was simply "Make sure you give away authentic affirmation and encouragement. And do it often."

What are you mumbling to yourself? Something about "What's the big deal? Everybody knows that!"

You're right. We all know that. The real dividing line comes between those of us who merely *know that* and the small handful of people who purposefully choose to *live that*. There's a huge difference there, my friend.

It usually won't come naturally.

If you really train yourself to mentally look for true, positive things about other people, you'll be blown away at how many good things you can come up with. Emerson once said, "Every man I meet is my superior in some way." If somebody like Emerson could say that, I don't think it should be too tough for us ordinary people to find qualities in others that we can authentically affirm. People are

SECTION 2: FRIENDSHIPS

naturally drawn to someone who sees the best in them and is secure enough to say it.

Now don't confuse authentic affirmation with phony flattery. There's a world of difference. All I'm saying is that if you teach yourself to consciously look for the best in others and then tell them about it, you will always have a circle of great friends. I should know. I have some of the greatest ones in all the world. Have I made you jealous yet? If so, just get to work yourself. You'll wind up having more amazing friends than you ever dreamed possible. I promise. It really is one of the most miraculous relationship secrets in the universe.

Thanks Joanie,
your friendship really does
mean the world to me.

Love,
J

"FRIENDS CAN BE LIKE ELEVATOR BUTTONS; THEY CAN EITHER BRING YOU UP OR TAKE YOU DOWN."

—UNKNOWN

Chapter 15

DO YOUR FRIENDS HAVE FLEAS?

OK. So if the truth be told, I'm not a dog lover. But my son, Justin, has a dog named "Jake." That was all great while Justin lived at home. The problem we face now is that Justin is an adult man who has moved out of the house. And sad to say, his living accommodations don't allow for pets. Are you getting the picture? I am now a devoted grandmother to this white dog named "Jake."

Jake has been helpful at times, I must admit. He's taught me some pretty important lessons. Less than a year ago, he started scratching and itching himself. Being the loving, caring "dog grandmother" that I am, I just let him itch for a few days. But Jake got even with me.

You see, one night I laid down on my living room carpet to read. (In case you're wondering, I share that same carpet with Jake.)

Moments after lying down on the floor, I began to itch...and itch...and itch. You can figure out the problem from there. A new "Mayo-ism" that was born that night: ("He who lies down with dogs shall rise up with fleas!")

Profound, don't you think? I do. Because it's true in the arena not of only dogs, but friends. You "catch" whatever "personality fleas" your friends have whenever you hang around them. Those "fleas" can come in the form of attitudes,

IF YOU HANG AROUND WOLVES, YOU'RE GOING TO LEARN TO HOWL.

priorities, dreams, and even words. But believe me on this one. Those "fleas" will invariably jump off your friends and onto you. The moral of my little story? Just make sure the friends you're hanging out with have the kind of "fleas" you want to be scratching!

The Scriptures often focus on the importance of choosing the right kinds of friends. So how long has it been since you asked yourself, "What direction are my friends taking me?" If your answer is neutral, I think you're wrong. Truth be told, the less you associate with some people, the more your life will improve. When my life and contentment start to unravel, it invariably involves a friendship that has had a negative impact on me in some way. If you hang around wolves, you're going to learn to howl. But if you hang around eagles, pretty soon you'll learn how to fly.

What did I hear you saying? You're lonely? I understand and I'm really sorry. But please hear me clearly. It is far better to be lonely than to hang around the wrong people. Just remember that eagles never flock. You have to find them one at a time. And that's true in life as well as in science. Besides, there are incredible positives that can come out of lonely seasons in your life. I often remind myself,

HUGE principle

"Loneliness becomes my friend when it forces me to draw companionship from God that I would like to draw from another human being." So it's really far better to temporarily be a little lonely than to cheapen yourself through wrong friendships.

I know. I can hear what you're thinking. You're saying, "No hurry. I can get out of this questionable friendship any time I want."

Think again, my friend. That's the same thing Samson said about his friendship with Delilah. But that friendship wound up costing him both his eyes and his destiny. Don't play the odds. Too much is on the line. Besides, if things get too tough, call me. I have a great dog named "Jake" who would love to keep you company.

"NOTICE YOUR FEMALE FRIENDS FOR THE RIGHT THINGS. SOMETIMES, EVEN IN THE CHURCH COMMUNITY, IT SEEMS LIKE BEING A 'GOOD GIRL' EARNS YOU NOTHING MORE THAN WALLFLOWER (PRUDE) STATUS."

16

14 THINGS GIRLS WISH GUYS KNEW ABOUT FRIENDSHIP

01. Don't send mixed signals to us. Since we are "just friends," please watch the amount of emotional energy you put into our relationship. Girls analyze everything. And if you give us emotional signals sometimes that we're "more than friends," we'll probably think you are interested in us.

02. Love us like a brother and give us the same emotional safety you would give your own sister. We girls are internally wired to appreciate it when a guy watches out for us, has our back, and does manly things for us. Unfortunately, many of us have not had close relationships with our dads or big brothers. So without sounding weird, it's really healthy for us to have some

guy-friends in our life who have pure motives and watch out for us.

03. **Don't treat us like "one of the guys" because we're not!** If you're smart, you'll also avoid inflammatory female jabs (even if they're funny to you) like, "What's wrong? Is it your time of the month?"

04. **Help us avoid making stupid mistakes with other guys.** Since you're a male yourself, you understand men better than we do. So if we start to be romantically interested in a guy who is a jerk, say something! Warn us (not out of romantic interest yourself but out of pure, brotherly protection).

05. **Remember that one of the greatest ways you show authentic friendship to us is by (listening when we talk.)** On the other hand, "talks" should not go too deep because wrong signals will easily be sent.

06. **Don't let your personal insecurities or hurts make you outwardly angry, defensive, detached, or arrogant.** Be man enough to fight through those feelings. When they do erupt onto the scene, have the courage to admit to us what's going on. (i.e. "Sorry I blew up last night and over-reacted. I'm just feeling pretty freaked out about my future, so I was on edge.")

You see, when you're strong enough to be honest with us about what's really going on inside of you, we'll march to the end of the planet for you. We just need you to let us know what you're thinking instead of always shutting us out. (All the movies and magazines that make it seem like girls always want men to be strong are *dead wrong*. Honesty carries a lot more weight with us than plastic, superficial machoism.)

07. **Make sure our friendship is two-sided.** Don't just prioritize our relationship when you need me to do research for your term paper, or fill up a lonely Saturday night. That's not called friendship. That's called being a user.

08. **Trust is a big deal to us.** So if I give it to you, don't violate it. That means guarding your emotions, remaining consistent, and keeping my confidences. No fair treating me like a sister six days out of the week and then like a girlfriend on the seventh. That becomes scary and unstable to us. Be one of those rare males who really cares about his female friends for what's inside of them, not for the "wrapping paper."

 09. **Encourage! Encourage! Encourage!** And try to drop the sarcasm too. Girls come alive when someone notices something they're doing

right and mentions it. So help us out with this one. Without being mushy, tell us occasionally what you appreciate about us. We know that sarcasm is almost a guy's second language in our culture. And we don't deny that sometimes you're really funny when you're sarcastic. But try to drop it in our friendship. Though we might laugh on the outside, it creates a less secure friendship dynamic on the inside. And though it probably goes without saying, if you have rotten language, drop it around us too. You make us feel cheap and dirty.

10. **Don't misread our friendship for something more.** Just like we don't want you to send mixed signals, we'll try to do the same. But please give us the fun of having guy friends without secretly reading other things into the relationship. If you start to have feelings, just level with us and back away.

11. **It is almost impossible for a guy and girl to be "best friends" without one of them internally having feelings for the other person.** So guard against the friendship being "too close." (Though we girls don't like to admit it, it's usually the female side of the equation that gets this "best friend" deal out of whack.)" No matter how many friendship or emotional needs the relationship might bring you, guard against the possibility of "unclear

intentions." It's no fair to use tender voice tones and words *Refer back to #1* when you're lonely and then later say, "I don't have a clue how she ever got that idea."

12. Notice us for the right things. Sometimes, even in the church community, it seems like being a

BE MORE THAN A FRIEND WHO IS CHRISTIAN...BE A CHRISTIAN FRIEND.

"good girl" earns you nothing but prude, wallflower status. It would be so great to feel like sharp guys honestly appreciate the fact that we prioritize character and integrity above sensuality and manipulation.

13. As our friend, give us hope that men of God really do still exist in today's culture. We aren't looking for perfection, but we want to believe that God really has a "knight in shining armor" somewhere on the planet for us. So model Christ-honoring character in front of us. You'll be giving us hope for the future and guarding our hearts against cheap, stupid choices in the present.

14. Be more than a friend who is Christian. Be a Christian friend. There's a world of difference. Occasionally, blow us totally out of the water by offering to pray with us about something. We know it can feel weird and awkward sometimes, but it will make you next in line to "Braveheart" if you do.

THERE'S A HUGE DIFFERENCE BETWEEN TWO PEOPLE WHO ARE BOTH CHRISTIANS AND FRIENDS AND TWO PEOPLE WHO ARE HONESTLY "CHRISTIAN FRIENDS."

BFF ☺

12 THINGS GUYS WISH GIRLS KNEW ABOUT FRIENDSHIP

01. It's exactly what it's called: a friendship. Nothing more! Nothing less. If a guy is interested in making a friendship romantic, he will let you know that. Please don't let your mind get carried away and emotionally make the friendship more than it is. That will wind up ruining our ability to have a great friendship totally.

02. Treat me like you would treat your brother. Maybe that's a cheesy way to define it, but I hope it gets the point across. Our society doesn't make it easy for a guy and girl to just be really good friends. People are always trying to make it more. But great guy-girl friendships will make both of our lives richer. If we both keep our heads on straight and our brains connected, we can have a great, long-term friendship. — *Please really get this one*

03. **Spare us from your "drama queen" moments.** That really drives us guys crazy. I know. I know. Girls are wired differently from guys, complete with high octane "feelers." But count us guys out when our friendship begins to be clouded with daily scenarios that feel like scripts from "Days of Our Lives."

It's also no fair to take things out on us when you're having "an emotional day." Go yell or pout at your cat or another female friend. Just please leave us out of the loop. You'll make everyone in your life much happier if you live by this simple mantra: Don't react. Respond.

04. **Don't hold grudges and keep bringing negative, hurtful things back up. Talk things over and then move on.** Also try to steer clear of the three-letter-cuss-word: "NAG." Someday when you're married, your husband will hate it if you nag him. So practice avoiding this form of communication in our friendship right now.

05. **Please don't make the mistake of falling in love with love.** It's tough to have a fun, healthy relationship with a girl who hasn't figured out that most guys aren't like the "Romeo's" they see in the movies. Try to remember that "Puppy love leads to a dog's life." We both started this thing as friends. Let's fight to keep it that way.

06. **Laugh with me, make me think I'm funny, and be fun yourself.** Call it male ego if you want, but all guys want girls to think that they're "the man." So laugh at our jokes (even when we're a little cheesy) and make us feel like you think we're pretty cool.

No "pity laughs" please

We really love it when you're fun too. Do some spontaneous things. Start a mud fight, go for a crazy marathon run around the park, or try throwing a picnic in the rain. Don't worry about how your hair will look or what will happen to your make-up. Just be fun and full of life. It makes you a friend we're proud to "do life" with.

07. **Don't send mixed signals to us. No fair using us for friendship when you can tell we are beginning to fall for you romantically.** Have the integrity to talk things over and be clear about what you want out of the friendship. You don't want us to use *you* during lonely seasons. So make sure you treat us with the same emotional integrity.

Big hint to female friends: If we try to kiss you, hold hands with you, or any related sorts of activities, we no longer think of you as just a friend. So no matter how good our emotional energy and attention feel at that moment, don't let it happen. *Don't be flattered— It won't last* If you do, you're playing with fire and probably allowing me

We stink at it (in a hormonal moment) to ruin a great friendship.

08. Don't expect us guys to read your minds. Girls are pretty good at this, but guys stink at this category. If you want us to know something, say it! When you're ticked with us, tell us. Sometimes you'll feel like we need a seeing-eye dog or something to help figure stuff out, but just be patient. And tell us what you're feeling! (Important hint: Try not to make every misunderstanding seem like a huge deal. If every week is another big deal, we'll back away from the friendship because we begin to feel we're on estrogen-overload.)

09. Get our backs, but don't talk behind our backs! Sounds a little contradictory, doesn't it? But both of these things are a big deal inside the male mind. We need to feel like a good female

GET OUR BACKS, BUT DON'T TALK BEHIND OUR BACKS!

friend has our back and helps look out for us (just like a good biological sister would). But we also need the confidence that if you get mad at us, you'll talk to us about it, not every girlfriend in your life. It turns us off when we become "public enemy #1" to your female friends because you get "diarrhea of the mouth" every time you get ticked with us.

10. **Even though we're just friends, remember that guys are still really visual.** If you dress like a flesh buffet, don't be surprised if we treat you like a piece of meat. OK, maybe a guy is supposed to be so strong that he never has these problems with a friend. But sorry, girls. That's just not reality. Please watch what you wear. *This is how you respect us.*

11. **Help me be the man of godliness and character I really want to be inside.** You might not hear me talk much about that. But it's probably because I feel like I've failed so many times in front of you that I'm embarrassed to let you know how I really feel inside.

Guys are hard on themselves. You may not know it, but we keep a mental scoreboard on ourselves and get pretty ticked when we don't live up to our own private standards. We hate it that our eyes sometimes wander to rotten sites on the Internet.

We ache when our self-discipline becomes so disgustingly weak—in lots of different areas.

So give us some hope. Try to catch us doing something good and Christ-honoring. Then sincerely tell us how much you appreciate that. Initiate talks with us about God because we'll probably be more hesitant to start those. (Remember? You're more comfortable verbally than most guys are).

Someone once said, "To a man is given the greater spiritual authority. But to a woman, the greater ability to influence." So with that in mind, use your female "ability to influence" to help us become more the man of God we really want to be.

> **TO A MAN IS GIVEN THE GREATER SPIRITUAL AUTHORITY. BUT TO A WOMAN, THE GREATER ABILITY TO INFLUENCE.**

12. **As I mentioned before, there's a big difference between two people who are Christians and friends...and two people who are honestly "Christian friends."** Let's pay the private prices to be the second. We'll both be better people for it. *Enough said.*

I THOUGHT YOU SAID YOU LOVED ME

CHEW AND SPIT ROMANCE

SOLO SEX

PORN-
THE MALE AND FEMALE KIND

13 WAYS
TO BEAT TEMPTATION

THE MASTERPIECE

This section is about as
"UNCENSORED"
as you are

SECTION 3

SEX

GUY
MEETS
GUY;
GIRL
MEETS
GIRL

WHAT
JERRY
SPRINGER
AND OPRAH
WON'T
TELL
YOU

SCRIPTURE
AMMO TO FIGHT
TEMPTATION

"ANYTHING YOU COMPROMISE TO GAIN, YOU WILL EVENTUALLY LOSE."

Chapter 18

I THOUGHT YOU SAID YOU LOVED ME

The car door shut behind her abruptly.

Leaning back down towards the window, she spoke softly. "I'm sorry tonight had to end like this."

The silence from the other side of the car was deafening. He was angry. He was frustrated. And he was embarrassed.

Coldly, right before he pulled his car away from her curb, he mumbled, "I thought you really cared about me." The shrill noise of his old muffler echoed through the neighborhood as he sped away. He pulled away before she could answer back.

Confused, she paused to re-think the evening. It had started so great. She really did care about him deeply. But in the last hour or so, things had gotten pretty heated. No, they weren't about to go to bed with each other. But his hands had gone to places on her body that she had privately marked off limits. Five minutes. Ten. Then twenty. The progression of events was not a pretty one. Finally she knew that if she didn't make a move to cut things off then, it would be nearly impossible in a few more minutes.

"Take me home," she said softly.

"Home? What are you talking about?" he said back in surprise.

"You know what I'm talking about. Neither one of us is strong enough to handle this tonight. I care about you too much to let us mess things up."

A little different from the culture's view of love

Ever been in a car where the silence was so thick that you felt you could cut it? That was the case that night.

Seconds passed. They seemed like awkward, chilly moments. "I thought you really loved me," he said. There was a strange edge in his voice. Part of it was almost pleading for response and the other part was angry over what felt like rejection.

"I do," she quietly spoke as she reached for the car door handle. "That's why I asked you to take me home."

Her last words that night were simple but profound. "Anything we compromise to keep, we will eventually lose"—and I care too much about our relationship to risk losing it." The door slammed behind her as some sort of punctuation mark. He and his noisy muffler made their exit from the neighborhood.

×   ×   ×

Strange how life works. Jesus says that anything we really want to keep, we have to (in some way) often lose. Maybe it's because He wants to make sure that that thing, desire, or person doesn't have an unhealthy degree of control over us.

WHAT ARE YOU HOLDING ON TO REALLY TIGHTLY?

So any time we compromise to hold on to something, we've already signed its inevitable death notice.

What are you holding on to really tightly? Your friends? Your job? Your sports career? All those are great things. But beware when the voices of compromise begin to cloud your related responses: your priorities, your focus, your thought-patterns. You find yourself beginning to rationalize things. (Know the definition of "rationalization"?

It's "the skin of a reason stuffed full of a lie.") Anyway, those rational-izing times are pretty pivotal. That's the moment that you need to be careful how big of a price you're willing to pay to hold on—no matter what you're grasping tightly to.

Decision points aren't easy. But most things in life that really count aren't. So try to remember these words the next time you're standing on a curb, listening to a friend's noisy muffler drive away: "Anything you compromise to gain or keep, you will eventually lose." Not sometimes. Not usually. But always.

"YOU ARE FREE
TO IGNORE THE
COMMANDMENTS
OF GOD, BUT NEVER
FREE TO AVOID THE
CONSEQUENCES."

WHAT JERRY SPRINGER AND OPRAH WON'T TELL YOU

- The stats are pretty scary: About 3 millions teenagers—one in every four sexually active youth in America—contract sexually transmitted diseases annually. (Keener Communications Groups, May 2002.)

- A December report by the Center on Addiction and Abuse at Columbia University found that 63% of all teenagers who use alcohol have also had sex. This figure is compared to 26% of non-drinking teenagers.

- The cyber-sex industry generates approximately $1 billion annually in pornography and is expected to grow to $5-7 billion in only the next 5 years. (National Council Report, 2002.)

- An article in *Seventeen* Magazine, "Teenagers Under Pressure," found that a majority of teens who were sexually active wish they had waited. Eight in ten girls said they wish they'd waited until they were older. Six in ten guys said they wish they had waited. (EDK Associates and the Ms. Foundation for Women.)

So what's your internal response to those numbers? If you've watched too much TV or listened to too much music, you numbly think, "That stuff will never happen to me." But you're wrong, my friend. You're wrong, that is, unless you realize that the best birth control method is still abstinence.

You: "'Abstinence?' Is that a word for a new computer program?"

Me: "No, it means you don't go to bed with anyone before you get married to them."

You: "I thought that went out with the Dark Ages. Do people actually live like that anymore?"

Me: "Not many, but the smart ones do. The list of benefits is pretty impressive. Besides that, God is really clear in His Word about this one. He says that sex is out until you're married."

You: "For real? Where in the Bible does it talk about staying out of bed with someone till you're married? That sounds pretty old-fashioned to me."

Me: "For starters, Ephesians 5:3, Colossians 3:5, and 1 Thessalonians 4:3. There are lots more if you're interested."

You: "Thanks, but that's OK. Why does God stick His nose into my business on all this anyway?"

Me: "To help you out. See, He created your body and your sex drive. So it stands to reason that He knows how it will operate best over the long haul. It's kind of like an automatic dishwasher that comes with an owner's manual. How stupid would it be for someone to throw out the instruction manual and insist on running the dishwasher his own way? Anyone with brains knows the manufacturer knows the best way to get the most positive results from the dishwasher. After all, the manufacturer made it. It's the same way with God and His directions to us about sex. He made the 'machinery' and so He's the expert on how it runs best!"

GOD NEVER CONSULTS YOUR PAST TO CREATE YOUR FUTURE.

Good thing

You: "OK...OK. So maybe the real problem isn't so much that I don't agree. Maybe the real truth is that I just don't know how to turn things around. You see, where do I go from here? Things are pretty messed up in my life right now in this arena."

The truth— for many of us

Me: "Thanks for the honesty. Let me give you some simple suggestions that could make a world of difference. They'll also be strategic for people wanting to dodge these challenges in their future."

Allow me to suggest a few steps to help you start an exciting "Chapter 2" in your life. I'm not saying that the journey to sexual purity will be an easy one. But I am saying that it will be one of the most crucial decisions you will ever make. I realize that some of you reading this chapter have already given up your virginity. Please just remember that God never consults your past to create your future. And to those of you who still remain virgins, remember that God's grace wants to help you continue this commitment right up to the marriage altar. Whatever your situation, let me give you a few suggestions:

01. Make some "pre-choice choices." (Another "Mayo-ism." Sorry.)

Weird phrase, I know. But I just want you to decide what sexual purity is going to look like for you. And I want you to decide that *now,* not when you're alone in a car with someone.

What's that? You say that you've already blown it big time in this area? Well, I have great news for you, my friend. The journey to purity can begin right now, right here. (Translation: Sincerely ask Christ for His forgiveness and then choose to draw a line in the sand and start fresh again. Does that work? You bet! The Bible says that if we confess honestly our sins, Christ is always faithful to forgive us and to cleanse us from all unrighteousness.)

Back to "pre-choice choices." I'm just suggesting that you need to make your decision now about how far you'll go. When you're alone with a person of the opposite sex, you'll have to make an obvious choice on what you will be OK with. But now, while the strength of your brain is still greater than your hormones, make specific "pre-choice choices." Decide in very clear, uncertain terms what your standards are going to be. After all, (not to decide is to decide.)

02. **Make a "Won't Do List" and make it embarrassingly specific.** I know it's a little awkward to write stuff like this down. But it's far better that you *write* it down than that you eventually have to *live* it down.

Let me give you a few suggestions to get you started:

"If I really like someone, kissing will be great. (If I make the person wait long enough to get it from me.) But I'm not going to have marathon kissing sessions with anybody—no matter how much I like them. I'm also not going to let hands go places on my (their) body that are covered by a bathing suit. (Note to self: Hands do not "slip." They know exactly where they are going.) I will not lay down with the other person or kiss them while in a prone position. Oral sex, tonguing, sucking, and licking are all out. I'll leave dental hygiene to the dentist. I'm also not going to tell someone of the opposite sex that I love them. I'm going to save those three words until I meet someone I date a long time and become very serious with. (Did I say *long* time and *very* serious?) When I finally give them those three words, it will be the secret signal between me and Jesus that I think this person is 'the one.'"

OK, it's your turn now. Pull out a sheet of paper and start writing out your "pre-choice choices."

Pre-Choices choices

Have you written down enough specifics that you are praying nobody else ever sees this sheet of paper? If not, keep writing and get more direct with your answers! If you're fighting with yourself about whether or not you should write something down, that's a good indication that you're in the middle of a war (a spiritual one, I mean).

Romans 7:19 (NLT) talks about it. Paul (a guy I relate to) says, "I want to do what is good, but I don't. I don't want to do what is wrong, but I do it anyway." Sound like anyone you know? At any rate, if you're fighting with yourself about writing one of your specific "no-no's" down, chances are you need to put it on the list.

03. **Decide what your fuse-shorteners are and determine to stay clear of them.** (Write this list down too. Call it your "Fuse-Shortener List.")

A FUSE SHORTENER IS ANY PERSON, PLACE, OR PATTERN THAT SHORTENS MY SEXUAL FUSE AND MAKES ME MORE VULNERABLE TO AN EXPLOSION OF TEMPTATION IN MY LIFE.

I often talk about "fuse-shorteners" when I talk about "pre-choice-choices." Let me explain where the phrase came from. I was hanging out with a couple of teenagers one evening around the Fourth of July. We drove past a fireworks display, and the guy got all excited. His car practically drove itself onto the lot.

Within a couple of minutes, I found myself in the middle of a pretty sensational fireworks demonstration. (It was obvious that the man running the fireworks stand had a little too much merchandise left. So, he put on a great show for us, hoping to convince my friend to buy more.) The result? It worked. My friend spent a lot of money that evening. Anyway, back to our story.

The couple and I went through a Sonic drive-thru before they dropped me off at my house. (I'm a Strawberry Limeade addict.) As I started to get out of the car, I laughingly told them, "Be good tonight, you two. And watch out for fuse-shorteners!"

The guy stuck his head out the window, smiled, and then said, "That's a new one. Want to help me understand?"

"Sure," I said. "The guy we just bought the fireworks from didn't make them all explode as soon as he lit the fuse. The explosion took time, depending on the length of the fuse. The point was, though, that once the fuse was lit, an eventual explosion was inevitable."

Being the good sport he was, the guy finished my new parallel. "So I suppose you're telling us to stay away from places that shorten our sexual fuse. I gotta give it to you, Jeanne. It's a different way to look at it."

We all laughed, the car sped off, and I was left with my own thoughts. *Fuse shorteners,* I thought to myself, *aren't just places. They can be any person, place, or pattern that shortens my sexual fuse and makes me more vulnerable to an explosion of temptation in my life.*

Then the news flash of the night hit me. Are you ready?

www.
Big deal.
com

THERE WILL OFTEN BE ABSOLUTELY NOTHING WRONG WITH THE ACTUAL FUSE-SHORTENER ITSELF. THAT'S WHERE PEOPLE GET TRIPPED UP. THEY SPEND THEIR ENERGY DEFENDING THE RIGHTNESS OF THE ACTUAL PERSON, PLACE, OR PATTERN INVOLVED. BUT YOU SEE, THE PROBLEM IS NOT SO MUCH CAUSED BY THE SPECIFIC FUSE-SHORTENER ITSELF— BUT INSTEAD BY WHERE THE FUSE SHORTENER CAN EVENTUALLY LEAD ME.

In other words, there may be absolutely nothing wrong with a certain location. But it becomes a fuse-shortener when I find myself more vulnerable to temptation when I hang out there. The same goes with different people in my life. They may all be awesome. But I need to be honest with myself about the kind of emotional energy they pull out of me. The same thing also applies to certain patterns in my life. Maybe listening to a certain type of music is not wrong in itself. But the question is, "Does this music fan positive attitudes in my life or more negative ones?"

Let me give you a hypothetical Fuse-Shortener List:

- Being alone in my bedroom with John (or anyone's bedroom of the opposite sex, for that matter).

- Listening to a certain type of music.

- Hanging out with Phil and Kari. (They're fun, but their standards make it easy for me to lower mine.)

- Disregarding the "HALT Principle." (The "HALT Principle" reminds us to "HALT" when we are Hungry, Angry, Lonely, or Tired.)

Put anything on your fuse-shortener list that is a person, place, or pattern that makes you more vulnerable to temptation. And remember, there may be absolutely nothing wrong with the fuse-shortener itself. That's (exactly what the enemy wants you to keep saying to yourself.) The danger comes in with where that fuse-shortener eventually takes you. At some point, with enough time and energy, a meltdown will be likely. Unless you come to terms with this kind of honest thinking, failure will be inevitable.

Note to self: The enemy doesn't care how long it takes to get you to mess up. He just wants to keep you slowly headed in the wrong direction. (It's called "The Slippery Slope." And man, is it slippery!)

Another note: The bad guy (i.e. the devil) patiently reserves the right to cash in on your compromise at his most opportune moment.

Now, before you leave step three, take the time to write all this out in a prayer of commitment to the Lord, asking for His help, telling Him what you will and won't do sexually, and admitting where your fuse-shorteners are. Make this written prayer pretty decent because when you begin to seriously date someone, I suggest that you show him or her your prayer. If they're not OK with everything you have written, get out of the relationship. After all, your commitment to Christ is a whole lot more important than your commitment to this loser! If he or she makes fun of your standards, that's another indication that you need to ditch the relationship as fast as you can.

As you end that relationship, the enemy will try to whisper in your mind, "Jesus has forgotten you." But let me tell you something to remember at those moments. Jesus has not forgotten you, my friend. He's only protecting you.

Need more encouragement? Try this one: He who stands for NOTHING falls for ANYTHING.

SIGN ON A DEPARTMENT STORE
SALES TABLE THAT SADLY
REMINDS ME OF PEOPLE WHO
COMPROMISE SEXUALLY:

"MERCHANDISE
SLIGHTLY USED.

GREATLY REDUCED
IN PRICE."

Remember? We are talking about steps to sexual purity

04. Go spend some money on yourself. I knew you'd like this step. For real, go buy something that you can keep as a personal token between yourself and the Lord of your commitment to walk in mental and sexual purity. It might be a cool ring, a bracelet, a necklace, or whatever. Just make it something you will be comfortable wearing all the time. Then every time you glance at it, it will be a secret reminder between you and the Lord of your commitment to Him in this arena. Even when you're not perfect, it will remind you to keep fighting.

Speaking of tokens, once I bought a four-inch plastic doll to hang on the rearview mirror of the car of a dating couple I was trying to help. The little doll had long blond hair like me, so I called her their "Jeanne Doll." Laughingly, I told the guy to hang the doll up on his rearview mirror and not do anything together in the car that they wouldn't want me to see. (I was trying to make my "Integrity Crusade" a little fun!)

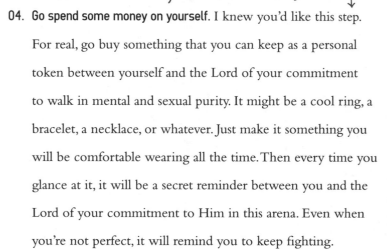

Anti-sin
Jeanne doll

The plan worked great for a few weeks. But one Saturday morning he dropped by the office to see me. His face had guilt written all over it. Finally I said, "Farley, what's wrong?"

FARLEY: "We messed up last night, Jeanne."

ME: "Tell me about it, my friend. What happened?"

FARLEY: (After sheepishly stuttering around for a while) "Well, I reached up and turned you around!" *(We laughed. Are you?)*

OK...OK...So tokens don't always work. But the ring really is a cool idea. So happy shopping. And while you're looking around at the mall, do some thinking about my words earlier in the book. "You're (free) to ignore the commandments of God, but never (free) to avoid the consequences."

The talk show hosts probably wouldn't agree with that statement. But believe me, my friend. This is the uncensored truth. And the Uncensored God we serve wants you to know that.

"YOUR MOST POWERFUL SEX ORGAN WILL ALWAYS BE YOUR MIND."

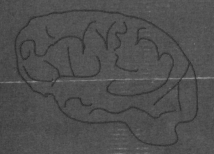

Chapter

20

SOLO SEX

It's about more than just what you're thinking...

HE WALKED INTO MY OFFICE and soberly handed me an envelope.

"Hi, Brent. What's this?" I asked casually. Brent was a leader in our youth group and one of the greatest guys around.

He cleared his throat nervously and struggled to give me eye contact. "It's...it's a letter of resignation."

"Resignation?" I said back, still not computing what was going on.

Brent's voice broke. "I'm an idiot, Jeanne. Don't make me talk about things now. I'm too embarrassed. Just know that I feel like a freak and a phony. It's a joke for me to stay in leadership around here. So there's my resignation."

"Brent, whatever's in this envelope, we'll figure it out. Why don't you sit down, and we can talk," I said compassionately. By this time, my friend was fighting to hide the tears that were starting to puddle inside his eye sockets.

"Later…later," he said quietly. "I can't talk about stuff right now. That's why I wrote the letter. Read it, and you'll understand."

Before I had time to respond, he slipped out of my office and closed the door behind himself. As it shut, I knew I needed to respect his need for privacy. So still confused, I opened up the envelope. Years have passed since that day, but the contents of the note remain painfully etched in my mind. In the letter, Brent shared about his own struggle with heavy masturbation—"solo sex." He talked about a pattern that had become so frequent and fantasy-driven that it had become a source of painful bondage for him. Let me reconstruct some of his words from the letter:

"…I hate myself. I know most guys deal with this. But it's slowly

⟶ **Does this sound familiar?**

become a monster in my life. Truthfully, I wouldn't want anyone to know the pictures that go through my mind while it's happening— or how many times a day I enter this secret world. I've tried to stop it or to at least slow it down. But I find myself failing over and over. That's why I've decided to step down from leadership. I just can't picture this as Christ-honoring in my life. Not this much. Not this often. Sorry I'm such a loser."

The whole topic of masturbation is a sensitive and yet key issue in today's society. Let's face it. We live in an oversexed world. You don't have to be Dr. Phil to figure out that this is a big deal in a lot of lives. Stats tell us that 95% - 98% of today's male culture deals with it on a regular basis and a lesser but still significant percentage of girls.

The challenge is that our culture clearly says, "No big deal. Have at it!" The church world, on the other hand, either pretends it doesn't exist, happily says "just do it in moderation," or makes participants feel like they will burn in a fiery hell if they give in. After working with thousands of teenagers and young adults for nearly forty years in youth ministry, I'm not sure that any of these responses reflect accurately the Father heart of God. So let me take a run at sharing my thoughts on this sensitive subject. Hopefully, you'll sense some balance.

Let me go to the bottom line first and then work backwards: Masturbation is a painfully common part of normal sexual development. But to allow yourself to repeatedly practice this pattern will create painful, long term results in your life. That's why God gives us the power in His Word to walk sexually free from this pattern. On the other hand,

Don't worry. I'll tell you how!

it's really important that Satan not be allowed to use this area to create devastating guilt and hopelessness in the lives of sincere believers. God is more interested in your (direction) than He is your (perfection.)

GOD IS MORE INTERESTED IN YOUR DIRECTION THAN HE IS YOUR PERFECTION.

So what's my take on this sensitive subject? Pursue mental and sexual purity with all your heart. Christ has provided all the power we need to walk in total freedom from masturbation. That's why you should whole-heartedly pursue purity with everything you've got. But along the journey, don't allow possible setbacks to be used by the enemy as tools of defeat, hopelessness, and discouragement.

SO WHAT PROBLEMS CAN "SOLO SEX" CREATE FOR ME?

Ever heard of "medial preoptic nucleus (MPN)"? Don't feel bad. Neither had I. Sounds like a disease or something, doesn't it? I studied some research done by a sexual addiction counselor named Dr. Douglas Weiss. That's where I learned that MPN is the center of your brain. (Are you impressed yet?)

At any rate, when you have any form of sexual release, your brain

Interesting huh? experiences a release of chemicals called endorphins and encephalin in the MPN. But hold on for this one. This surge of chemicals you get is the highest rush in the human body. The MPN is the same area that cocaine affects. (That's why cocaine is so quickly addicting.)

YOU BEGIN TO LOSE YOUR ABILITY TO BOND WITH REAL PEOPLE IN THE REAL WORLD. EVEN MORE SERIOUS, YOU BEGIN TO LOSE YOUR ABILITY TO BOND WITH ONE VERY IMPORTANT PERSON— YOUR FUTURE SPOUSE.

Because the physical reward (via the endorphins and encephalin) is so strong and powerful, it obviously makes you want to do it again…and again. But here's the scary catch: When you get the sexual sensation, whatever you are looking at (even in your imagination) begins to strongly bond with you. Put another way, when you masturbate, you are starting a process in your brain that actually bonds you to the fantasy world that is in your mind.

What's the big deal? Plenty. You begin to lose your ability to bond with real people in the real world. Even more serious, you begin to lose your ability to bond with one very important person—your future spouse. Instead, your bonding is towards a fantasy world that doesn't really exist. You're messing things up for yourself big time as you approach your future. Slowly, you also begin to see women (or men) as objects, not people. That's obviously not the way God created us to be. He wants us to have this kind of bond with only one person in our life—someone we will cherish as our marriage partner and closest friend, not a mere sexual object.

Dr. Weiss concludes his comments by saying: "Your brain doesn't know the difference between the sex-object being appropriate or inappropriate. It just knows it got the rewards." Now, if you get good stuff (chemical rewards) attached to bad things, what will your brain want to do? Bad things. So protect your brain. It's a holy place. If you start masturbating and move into fantasy or pornography, you will damage your life. It greatly affects your long-term sexuality and wholeness.

So keep reading!
The next few pages start
to give you some help...

Choose or lose!

HOW DO I BEGIN TO MAKE CHANGES?

SO GLAD YOU ASKED....

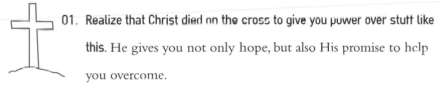

01. **Realize that Christ died on the cross to give you power over stuff like this.** He gives you not only hope, but also His promise to help you overcome.

02. **Begin to see purity as a virtue to be cherished, not a bunch of rules to be endured.** Christ calls us to purity in His Word because He created our sexual organs and knows how they will best operate. He wrote the "Operational Manual." We'd be pretty stupid not to study it carefully if we want long-term satisfaction. So embrace purity as something important and admirable, not something legalistic or warped.

03. **Recognize self-discipline as an important "muscle."** If you build it up now, you'll be able to use it in thousands of positive ways to create true happiness in your future. If you let yourself remain lazy and hormonally driven, you will pay the painful price later. Pay now or pay later.

156

Granted, self-discipline in this area is not always an easy one

to cultivate. But if teenagers and young adults can't control their

impulses before marriage, why would they be able to control them-

selves after they are married? There's sure nothing about a wedding

ceremony that magically gives a person self-control. That important

"muscle" has to be exercised in order to become strong. People often

Don't trick yourself into thinking

think that marriage will automatically take away the masturbation *your wedding day*

will break these habits

challenge. So sorry. It might for the first three months; but after that, *in your life*

you'll find yourself fighting the same old patterns. And the agonizing

truth is that often, no human companion can live up to the person

you've created in your fantasy world. ⟶ *WOW!*

04. **Read "The List: 13 Ways To Beat Temptation" at the end of this**

section. All those principles apply big-time here. Pay special

attention to removing the "fuse shorteners" that surround your

temptations regarding "solo sex." It's really important that you

identify specific times of the day and locations where you're

more tempted to masturbate. Then prayerfully prepare yourself

before these specific times. Don't play the mental game of, "I'll

touch myself but won't climax."

05. **Read over (and maybe even memorize) the key Scriptures given**

in "Scripture Ammo To Fight Temptation" at the end of this section.

Roll those Scriptures over in your mind as you fall asleep.

Consider sleeping with your bedroom door open.

06. Be especially disciplined about key problem times and places. Get out of bed in the morning as soon as you wake up instead of allowing your mind to wander. Be disciplined about the stuff you read in the bathroom and how much time you spend there. Be brutally honest with yourself about your TV, movies, and magazines. Stay off the late-night TV entertainment as you're starting to drift into sleep. When you're tired, you're weak. Stay away from stuff that makes you more vulnerable.

People struggling with alcohol wouldn't do well spending free time in a liquor store... Same principle applies here

07. Get yourself an accountability partner of the same sex. Remember that "lone rangers are dead rangers." So much freedom will come when you honestly share your struggle with another person you can trust. Then ask them to hold you accountable and ask how you're doing. (If you want this accountability stuff to really work, don't make the other person have to chase you down to ask how you're doing. Accountability without pre-established weekly check-in times where you initiate the contact usually is a joke.)

BIG ONE: IF YOU'RE WEAK IN THIS AREA AND TRYING TO CHANGE, AVOID THE "LADDER MENTALITY."

OK, you're right. It's another "Mayo-ism." But let me explain what I mean.

It's easy for the enemy to really twist things mentally with this one, especially if you are the conscientious type. You see, he depicts holiness to you as a super tall ladder. The mind games go kind of like this: Each time you make it through another day of overcoming in this area, you see yourself climbing up another step on the ladder.

But if you mess up or stumble, the enemy makes the whole thing feel incredibly hopeless. It's not like you've fallen a step or two. Instead, the enemy makes you feel like you've completely wiped out and fallen all the way to the very bottom of the ladder. That's how he tries to make the journey towards sexual purity and freedom seem so hopeless and discouraging. How many times can you fall to the bottom of the ladder without finally giving up totally and thinking the climb is hopeless? The obvious result is a part of the enemy's game plan: The sincere person who is pursuing mental and physical purity often finally gives up. (Remember Brent—the guy who delivered his resignation letter to me? That's the game the enemy tried to play on him.)

 But start smiling! Let me give you huge, big news: One "mess up" doesn't begin to cancel out all your previous sincere efforts. Contrary to what the enemy wants you to think, you're nowhere close to the "bottom of the ladder" where you *Really a big deal* feel like you have to start all over again. Like I mentioned earlier, the Lord's focus is not on perfection, but rather on direction. This whole process is really like a marathon race. You will probably fall down often. But instead of going back to the starting line, you just get back up and begin running again. (Remember: Falling down indicates movement. So congrats! At least you're going somewhere.)

Little by little, you will gain freedom in this area that you never thought possible. Be sure to use the Scriptures I give you in "Scripture Ammo To Fight Temptation." Romans 12:2 promises that you will begin to be "transformed by the renewing of your mind" as you read over those Scriptures daily. It works. I promise.

WISDOM FROM IMPORTANT CHRISTIAN PSYCHOLOGIST GURU,

Dr. James Dobson

EVER HEARD OF DR. JAMES DOBSON and Focus on the Family? He's a big deal. I researched with deep respect and interest his thoughts on this sensitive subject. He clearly encourages young men and women to steer clear. Yet he also shares his belief that haunting guilt and shame over this area has driven more young men away from Christ than almost anything else in the church world. *How you're doing in this area is not the key factor in how you + God are doing.*

So what's his message? Fight this pattern with all you've got. Grab onto Christ's authority and power to walk in mental and sexual freedom. But as you do that, don't let this one area become "ground zero" for your holiness and pursuit after Christ. This is not your primary measurement for how you and God are doing. If you make this area your "key righteousness barometer," you could be giving the enemy unnecessary ground in your life.

So that's it for this topic. Can you believe we did a whole chapter on masturbation?

I told you we'd earn the title of *Uncensored*.

"GUARD YOUR HEART
ABOVE ALL ELSE,
FOR IT DETERMINES
THE COURSE
OF YOUR LIFE."

PROVERBS 4:23 (NLT)

Chapter

21

THE MASTERPIECE

ONE EVENING WHEN I WAS SPEAKING to several hundred teenagers and young adults, I decided to do something a little strange. I opened my talk by passing out small cardboard boxes to everyone in the audience. You could just hear the undercurrent of sarcasm: "Gee, thanks, Jeanne. What a great gift. A cardboard box!"

To make matters more challenging, I made only one statement while the boxes were being passed out. I said firmly, "Don't look inside this box. Whatever you do, do *not* take the top off and look inside."

You're one of those people who would open the box, aren't you?!?

OK…So now I had really created a pretty awkward atmosphere in the auditorium. I passed out hundreds of cardboard boxes to my audience and then had the nerve to tell them to not look inside.

After the boxes were all passed out, I did something else pretty unusual. I looked around the auditorium, told everyone thanks for showing up, and then walked off the platform. Right before I disappeared from sight, I repeated my instructions one final time: "Please remember, whatever you do, don't open the box!"

I disappeared, and for the next few seconds, the auditorium grew very quiet. Then people started laughing and talking. What do you suppose everyone wanted to do? They all wanted to open the box! And when human nature took over and most everyone followed their instincts, they found that the cheap cardboard boxes were absolutely EMPTY! What a stupid, confusing thing for any speaker to do! The advertisements about the night had said that Jeanne Mayo was going to share on God's view of sex, and so the crowd was a large one. (It usually is when that's the topic.) But now, all I had done was to pass out empty boxes, tell them not to open them, and then disappear!

Hiding behind the stage curtain, I let the awkward, box-opening time continue until I saw that a couple of people were standing up to leave the auditorium. Then I grabbed the microphone again and made a quick re-appearance on the stage.

The crowd had mixed emotions as I started to talk. "Excuse me. If everybody could just sit back down, I'll explain what's going on here. You see, it was advertised that I was going to share tonight on God's view of sex. And what you just experienced emotionally represents the false concept some of you have about God's attitude and commandments in this area."

"We think of God as a Cosmic Killjoy," I continued. "We think He passed out sex to the human race and then said to all the single people in the earth, the contents in this box are incredible. But too bad for you single people. Make sure you don't open it up! Ha! Ha! Good luck trying to survive till you're married!"

> **THERE'S A HUGE DIFFERENCE BETWEEN THE MINDSET THAT SAYS, "YOU CAN'T HAVE THAT," AND THE MINDSET THAT SAYS "THIS IS UNIQUELY YOURS. GUARD IT CAREFULLY."**

"But you see, that's not God's attitude at all." The crowd was quiet now. Holding their little cardboard boxes, I knew they would remember the evening. I kept talking. "Instead, God passed out sex to the human race and said, 'I made the contents inside this box just for you. So guard it carefully. Keep it pure and safe. Don't let anyone open up this priceless gift I've given you until you do it in the sacredness of marriage.'"

With that perspective in mind, our human response should be something like, "This is my special box, made just for me by my heavenly Father. And I'm going to guard this box—big time. Nobody's messing with *my* box!"

That's why the Scriptures say in Hebrews 13:4, "Guard the sacredness of sexual intimacy between wife and husband" (MESSAGE). There's a huge difference between the mindset that says, "You can't have that," and the mindset that says, "This is uniquely yours. Guard it carefully."

When we think that God's attitude towards sex is just one of warped rules and hard-to-follow commandments, it's only human nature for us to want to rebel. But when we realize that He loves us so deeply that He wants us to guard our sexuality so it can bring us the most fulfillment, that's a whole different perspective. Instead of internally (and maybe unconsciously) rebelling against that commandment, we find ourselves being motivated to follow it.

This is a healthy, new perspective I hope you catch!

As I concluded my talk that evening, my mind raced back to an elderly man who told me years ago that sexual intimacy was kind of like sod. "Sod belongs in a yard," he said. "Take it out of its place, and it's not much more than dirt."

"Sex is the same way," the old man continued. "It's beautiful only when it's in its place, and that's inside marriage."

Before I concluded my talk that night, I did two last things. I passed out tiny little heart-shaped padlocks and keys to everyone in the crowd. "Put this padlock inside the box," I quietly instructed them. "And use it as a personal reminder of God's instruction to us in Proverbs 4:23 (NLT). It reads, 'Guard your heart above all else, for it determines the course of your life.'" Then I closed out the night with a story I heard years ago titled, "The Masterpiece." (A Christian communicator named Joshua Harris told it.) Let me wrap up this chapter by sharing it with you. It reflects God's tender, loving attitude towards sexual purity and the resulting huge benefits to us. So, grab a cup of coffee and make yourself comfortable. You're going to want to remember this one—I promise. It's uncensored truth at its finest.

It's a GREAT story

THE PARABLE OF
THE MASTERPIECE

There was once a brilliant artist who spent his life creating paintings of immeasurable value. People from all over the globe came to admire and bid for his priceless work. This magnificent artist had three sons, all three young men whom he loved deeply. But finally, the time came for the three young men to leave home.

The father, caring so much for the future happiness and fulfillment of his three sons, gathered them together. As a farewell gift, he presented each of his sons with a copy of his most priceless painting. He referred to the work of art as "His Masterpiece." The priceless gifts, though, came with only one very solemn instruction from the father. He told each of his beloved sons that the masterpiece he had created for each one of them was to only be seen and enjoyed by one other person in the whole world. That person was to be each son's future wife.

167

Lovingly, the father hugged each one of his sons farewell. As they left his home, each with the priceless painting, they heard the father calling out from the doorway: "(Protect) the painting. (Guard) it. Cher-ish it. So one day, when you experience it with the woman you make your own, you will have all the joy and fulfillment it can bring to you. To use it in any other way will greatly cheapen its worth and value." Each son promised his father to cherish the gift he had given him. Each one left, fully intending to follow his directions for the priceless paintings.

But the years wore on. And the three sons began to have differ-ent attitudes towards the paintings and the words of their father. The first son began to secretly resent the conditions of the painting. It just didn't make any sense to him. *After all,* he thought to himself, *the painting is so beautiful that I need to share it with other people. My father's instructions were born out of his culture and a different mindset. None of that relates to me right now.* (My father is just old-fashioned.) Sound familiar?

Sure enough, the first son soon developed a close relationship with a young woman. As the relationship deepened, he eventually showed her his Masterpiece. After all, this was his way of showing her how truly special she was to him. The young woman was blown away by the beauty of the work of art. But somehow, the first son never even bothered to tell her that it was a gift from his father. Instead, he took total credit for the Masterpiece himself.

Soon, though he had vowed it would never happen, the first son became tired of his female companion. So he began to show his Masterpiece to many other women. Over time, the whole experience became no longer special at all. In fact, sharing his Masterpiece became very, very common. The deep joy of this intimate sharing began to fade away. The first son wondered what had changed. *Perhaps,* he thought to himself, *the women I am sharing it with are not as special as the first ones.* Whatever the cause, he simply knew that things had slowly changed.

Months and years passed by. A layer of dirt began to slowly cover the Masterpiece, dulling it from its original beauty. Because it was not being carefully protected, countless fingerprints began to cause more distortion to its worth. Over time, the elements of life even began to crack and decay the painting.

Unexpectedly one day, the father arrived to visit his son. He was horrified at what had happened to his gift. The words of the master painter were heartbroken but stern to his son: "You have not protected and guarded the Masterpiece as I have asked you to do. So you have brought your punishment upon yourself. It is not one that I ever desired for you. You will live the rest of your life without the fullest measure of pleasure and enjoyment from my Masterpiece."

Stopping to choke back his heartbroken tears, the father concluded by saying softly, "If only you would have listened to me, my son. I asked you to guard my gift with all diligence. But you did not obey my words."

The second of the three sons had a different story with his cherished painting. He thought to himself, "If my father has told me to guard this as a secret only for my future wife, there must be something very bad and shameful about the painting itself." So the second son found a place to hide the painting away, in a back closet of a room which was never visited or spoken about. Though he never admitted such, it seemed that the second son was truly embarrassed about the Masterpiece.

Years later, this son did marry a special young woman. Remembering his father's directions, on his wedding night, he escorted his bride into the dark closet where the picture had been hidden. But instead of sharing the Masterpiece with her in joy, he embarrassingly opened the door for her to experience it. As quickly as possible, though, he slammed the door again. Never did the second son mention to his bride that the painting was a treasured gift from his father for their marriage. As a matter of fact, the painting was rarely revisited.

When the father appeared at their home, his reaction was once again a painful one. Instead of praising the second son for his hiding of the Masterpiece, he shook his head in disbelief. ("I gave this to you as a cherished gift—not something for you to be ashamed of.) You and your wife were to enjoy the beauty of this Masterpiece together. It was to make your love for each other even stronger. But instead, you treat my gift as though it were something evil and dirty. Just like your first brother, you have broken my heart by dishonoring my gift to you."

Now the third son, like the other two, had accepted the painting and was awed by its beauty. But he understood the deep need to guard it—to cherish it—until the day he married his future bride. So he took the painting to his new home and found the perfect room for it. He carefully hung it up and then thought to himself, "My father is right. The beauty of this painting will be most magnificent when I save it and share it only with my future wife." So the third son shut the door to the art room, locked it, and put the key around his neck for safe-keeping.

GUARD YOUR HEART ABOVE ALL ELSE, FOR IT DETERMINES THE COURSE OF YOUR LIFE.

Years and years passed by. At times, he was tempted to show others the Masterpiece because he did not find his bride as quickly as he thought he would. But he refused to weaken. The key to the room remained around his neck, near his heart. At long last, he met the princess of his life. On the first night that they were married, he walked her with pride and deep love to the door where the Masterpiece had been kept. Slowly, he took the key from around his neck and opened the door. Together, for the first time, they walked together inside the sacred room. They were without words as they experienced the beauty of their father's Masterpiece—together—for the first time.

Upon their father's arrival, his heart swelled with joy. "You have honored me," he said to them. "You have taken delight in my Masterpiece. You have guarded it and treasured it through the years, though I know that it has been very difficult at times. But now, your reward is that the beauty of your Masterpiece will not fade with time. Instead, because you have guarded it, the Masterpiece will only grow in its beauty as your commitment to each other grows through the years."

And so as legend has it, the marriage of this third and final son was one of the most special unions ever known to mankind. Though it was costly, this son had chosen to guard his father's Masterpiece. And because of that, he spent a lifetime reveling in the joy and fulfillment of its beauty.

He had heeded the instruction of his father, instructions echoed by a wise man named Solomon in Proverbs 4:23 (NLT): "Guard your heart above all else, for it determines the course of your life."

"RIGHT CHOICES
EVENTUALLY
BRING
RIGHT EMOTIONS."

22

PORN—THE MALE
AND FEMALE KIND

LET ME TELL YOU A PARABLE called "The Dragon of Imagination."
It was adapted from a book entitled *Pure Desire* written by Ted
Roberts.[8] Take time to read it. I promise you'll be glad.

There was once a great and noble King whose land was terrorized

by a crafty dragon. Like a massive bird of prey, the scaly beast loved to

destroy villages with his fiery breath. Hopeless victims ran from their

burning homes, only to be snatched into the dragon's claws. Those

devoured instantly were more fortunate than those carried back to

the dragon's den to be devoured slowly, at his leisure. The King led

his sons and knights in many battles against the dragon. One day, the

unimaginable occurred.

Riding alone in the forest, one of the King's sons heard his name purred low and softly. In the shadow of the trees, curled among the boulders, lay the dragon. The creature's eyes locked with the prince, and the dragon's mouth stretched into a friendly smile.

"Don't be afraid," said the dragon. "I am not what your father thinks."

Lies come in all shapes and sizes

"Then what are you?" the prince asked.

"I am pleasure," said the dragon. "Ride on my back, and you will experience more than you ever imagined. So join me now. I will not hurt you. I'm only looking for a friend, someone to share fights with me. Have you ever dreamed of flying? Ever longed to soar in the clouds?"

Visions of soaring high above the hills drew the prince slowly from his horse. The dragon uncurled one great webbed wing to serve as a ramp onto his ridged back. Between the spiny parts of the dragon's back, the prince found a secure seat. Then the creature snapped his powerful wings twice and launched them together into the sky. The prince's fear began to melt into awe and excitement at what he began to feel and see.

From then on, the young prince met the dragon often, but secretly. He knew he could never tell his father, brothers, or the knights that he had befriended the enemy. The prince felt separate from them all. Their concerns were no longer his concerns. Even when he wasn't with the dragon, he spent less time with those he loved and more time alone.

The skin on the prince's legs became calloused from gripping the back of the dragon, and his hands grew rough and hardened. He began wearing gloves to hide the sickness. After many nights of riding, he discovered scales growing on the backs of his hands as well. With dread, he realized what his long-term fate would be if he chose to continue.

Finally, he resolved to return no more to the dragon. But after only a few days, he again sought out the dragon, having been tortured with desire. And so it happened time and time again. No matter how determined he was to break free, the prince eventually found himself pulled back, as if by the cords of an invisible web. Silently, patiently, the dragon always waited…until he had him in his grip again.

One cold, moonless night their trip took them to a sleeping village. Torching the roofs with fiery blasts from his nostrils, the dragon roared with delight as the terrified victims ran from their burning

homes. Yes, night after night, families and lives were being destroyed

by these rides of unbridled lust. The prince closed his eyes tightly in

an attempt to shut out the screams. Horrified, he recognized some of

the voices. They were his friends—his family. What agony to know

that his secret rides with the dragon were now hurting others he

cared about.

In the predawn hours, when the prince crept back from his dragon

rides, the road outside his father's castle usually remained empty. But

not tonight. Terrified refugees streamed into the protective walls of

the castle. "One of your sons was there!" one woman cried out. "I

saw him on the back of the dragon." Others nodded their heads in

angry agreement.

There's no such thing as hiding forever

Horrified, the prince soon found himself trapped. He looked up,

straight into the face of his father, the King. The King's face mirrored

the agony of his people as his eyes painfully met his son's. The prince

frantically began to run, hoping to escape into the night. But the

palace guards caught him and arrested him like a common thief.

They brought him to the great hall where his father sat solemnly on

the throne. The people on every side screamed against the prince.

"Banish him!" he heard one of his own brothers angrily cry out. "Burn him alive!" other voices shouted.

As the King rose from his throne, bloodstains from the wounded people glared darkly off his royal robes. The crowd fell silent to listen to his words. The prince, who could not bear to look into his father's face, stared at the blood-stained floor.

"Take off your gloves and your jacket," his father, the King, commanded. The prince obeyed slowly, dreading to have his sick ugliness uncovered before the whole kingdom. Wasn't this punishment enough? He had hoped for a quick death without further humiliation. Sounds of repulsion rippled through the crowd at the sight of the prince's thick, scaled skin and the hardening scales where once his backbone had been.

The King walked slowly toward his son. The prince steeled himself, fully expecting a harsh back-handed blow even though he had never been struck before by his father. Instead, his father embraced him and wept as he held him tightly. In brokenhearted disbelief, the prince buried his face in his father's shoulder. He wept uncontrollably.

His father at last spoke to him. "Do you wish to be free from the dragon, my son?"

The prince answered through his tears. "I have wished it time and time again, Father, but there is no hope for me."

"Not alone," said his Father, the King. "You cannot win this battle against the dragon alone."

"Father, I am no longer worthy to be your son. I am half beast," sobbed the prince. "Look at the horror and ugliness that now cover me."

A real dad can always see the real person inside....

But his father replied, "My son, my blood still runs in your veins. My love has always been stamped deep within your soul."

With his face still hidden tearfully in his father's embrace, the prince heard the King instruct the crowd. "The dragon is crafty. Some fall victim to his tricks and some to his violence, but there will be mercy for all who wish to be freed. Who else among you has ridden the dragon?"

The prince lifted his head to see someone emerge from the crowd. To his amazement, he recognized his older brother, a man who had been praised for his victories against the dragon in battle and for his many good deeds. Others came, some weeping, others hanging their heads in shame. The King embraced them all.

"This is our most powerful weapon against the dragon," he announced. "Truth." No more hidden flights. Alone we cannot resist him. But together, clinging to the power of My Cross, we will slowly find the needed grace and power. One day at a time, we will learn to walk free again—free from the dragon of our imagination."

Quite a parable, don't you think? Let me translate this "dragon" into the real world for you. It's a "ride" I would sure like to help keep you from—or at least shorten.

Imagine yourself in a world where the most gorgeous (or handsome) bodies in the universe are all coming after you! They never make demands. They never get in a bad mood. They never even have a bad hair day. They have perfect bodies and perfect willingness any time you decide to meet them.

Welcome to the world of porn. It can seem pretty harmless. After all, what's going on is just between you and the computer screen, you and the magazine, or you and cable TV. But I promise you that it is everything but harmless and everything but private. The impact of this pattern is shaping your future life in heavy, serious ways. Let me explain.

Dr. Judith Reisman tells us that porn slowly creates an agonizing "brain makeover." She explains from the world of neuroscience that pornographic visual images both quickly imprint and alter the brain by triggering an instant, involuntary, but lasting biochemical memory trail. This is true of "soft porn" as well as hard-core porn. Scientists say that in only 3/10 of a second, a visual image passes from the eye to our brain. The brain is then structurally changed, and memories are created. We are literally giving ourselves a lasting "brain make-over" with each visual experience we involve ourselves in. That's why the images are so tough to get rid of.

That's why the world of porn is guaranteed to mess up your future sex life. Porn numbs and desensitizes you sexually. You privately hide yourself away, hoping no one will disturb your fantasy world. One-dimensional women (or men) become your companions while slowly, your insides start to gnaw with a see-saw of guilt and passion.

Then one day, the scene changes. You enter the real world. It's your wedding day, and someone you deeply care about meets you at the end of the aisle. But the dream day doesn't have such a perfect ending. Why? Because that partner can never hope to measure up to the hotties you have been hanging out with in your fantasies. They're not airbrushed to make every feature and curve perfect. They are real people, with moods, feelings, fears, and even fat cells. What's the common ultimate outcome? You soon find yourself in a room again alone, making love with a person who doesn't even exist. And little by little, all possibility of having a fulfilling, healthy romance with someone you deeply care about slips further and further away from you. Sound exaggerated? It's not. Believe me. I've lost track of the number of destroyed relationships I have watched follow this agonizing pattern.

WE ARE LITERALLY GIVING OURSELVES A LASTING "BRAIN MAKEOVER" WITH EACH VISUAL EXPERIENCE WE INVOLVE OURSELVES IN.

I asked some people who are living with this challenge what they wish someone had said to them—earlier. Let me pass on their advice to you. These are actual quotes from some pages of advice they wanted you to hear. They're hoping that their gutsy honesty will help some of you:

01. **Tell them to take this fight seriously—the sooner, the better.** When you're dealing with porn, the passing of time becomes your enemy. It will be way, way harder to fight for change a year from now than it is right now.

02. **Guard your eyes. They really are the gateway to your soul.** 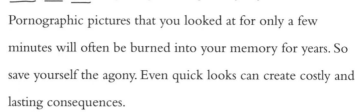 Pornographic pictures that you looked at for only a few minutes will often be burned into your memory for years. So save yourself the agony. Even quick looks can create costly and lasting consequences.

03. **Swallow your pride and get an accountability partner of the same sex.** You're going to have a tough time changing this one on your own. Realize that 47 percent of Christians surveyed said that pornography is a major problem in their lives. So you're not alone, and you're not some dirty, cheap person. But fight it now, or that is exactly where you're headed—very alone, very dirty, and very cheap.

Remember—Truth is where the change comes in

04. **Reach out to help others of the same sex who are struggling with this area.** Have the guts to ask friends how they're honestly doing. Then fight this thing together. If you don't struggle yourself but you are trying to help someone else, have the courage to often ask them how things are going. They will maybe feel too embarrassed to bring the subject up often. But everything inside of them is really screaming out for help.

05. **Know your vulnerable times.** If that's being on your computer after 9 at night, determine not to do it. Figure out your fuse-

shorteners, and have the brains to fight against them. This kind of compromise doesn't just happen. So iden-

FIGHT FOR YOUR FUTURE HAPPINESS AND YOUR FUTURE FAMILY.

tify what is leading up to some of the times when compromise screams the loudest. For most of us, there are small compromises (in our fantasy life, our TV watching, our music, or reading material) that slowly make us vulnerable on bigger battlegrounds.

06. **Be honest with yourself about the impact of masturbation.** It's not OK to engage yourself sexually while fantasizing about porno-graphic stuff you've looked at. Fight for your future happiness and your future family. No one can do it but you.

07. **Make up your mind that no technological convenience is worth messing up your entire life and your eternity with Christ.** Be willing

a.k.a. "fuse shorteners"

to take radical action if necessary. Disconnect your cable. Stay away from chat rooms or specific kinds of surfing. Maybe just go online only when other people are in the room.

08. **If stuff online has become a problem, watch how much time you spend on the Internet, period.** When you're lonely, depressed, or vulnerable, have the integrity to stay offline totally. Always go

online with a purpose. If the Internet has become almost a mindless entertainment activity where your brain goes into neutral and your defenses go down, realize that you're in dangerous territory. Even if you're not struggling with Internet porn now, realize that your mindset and time investment could easily lead you in that direction. Again, cut back on the time you spend on the Web, and make sure it always has a specific point. There are just far too many dark corners on the Web for you to aimlessly wander there for long periods of time and not think you'll find yourself in trouble. Avoid lingering on certain My Space pages where airbrushed hotties scream for your attention and solicit your dating service business.

09. **Prioritize "The List: 13 Ways To Beat Temptation" towards the end of the book.** I'm not saying any of this stuff is easy. I'm just saying that it works. There's only one problem. That list will only work on your life if *you* do.

10. **Let the Word of God become your new Best Friend.** Grab onto some of the Scriptures given here and read them over on a daily basis (hourly, if you need to). We give you a list of Scripture ammo at the end of this section. Use it. No one can fight

for you but you. Wake up and realize that the consequences are too big to be stupid about this whole thing.

11. **Remember that Christ's Word doesn't tell us to resist sexual tempta-tion. It tells us to flee from it.** In your private moments, don't let

"Run, Forrest, Run!"

yourself go places you shouldn't be and then try to tell yourself to "stand strong." Stay away in the first place.

12. **Realize that Christ's love will always outlast your sin. You won't feel like you deserve forgiveness, especially when you're repent-ing for the one millionth time about this.** But remind yourself that you never could have *deserved* Christ's forgiveness the very *first time* you blew it. So refuse to believe the lies from the enemy. Christ in you is bigger than all of this. Just don't allow your guilt to push you further away from Christ at the very moment you need Him the most. Remember that if Jesus really is all-knowing, He died for your first sin and knew about your last. So no matter how bad things get, you're not scaring Him away.

SO WHAT AM I CALLING "FEMALE PORN"?

Realize that the stats clearly tell us that lots of girls have the same struggles with porn that their male counterparts deal with. Girls deal with a secondary twist though in their battle against porn. Their porn often focuses on the romantic more than the sexual. Remember? Girls want to be rescued and taken care of. So if we view porn as anything that steadily creates an unreal, fantasized picture of the opposite sex in our minds, we've really opened up a whole panorama of stuff.

I'm not saying to pitch all "chick flicks," sappy music, girl magazines, or romance novels. I'm just saying that you're in trouble when you begin to mentally create a picture of some made-up guy who doesn't really exist. Real guys are not always amazing heroes. In the real world, they pass gas and don't usually send you roses. They can't read your thoughts across a crowded room and then magically make everything perfect again. So stop filling your head with pictures of guys who don't really exist. Your emotional address will be "Depression City" if you do.

Whether you're a guy or a girl, porn is a dragon you don't want to ride. Yes, it's one of the easiest and most private sensual rides you can take. But just remember one thing. It's also one of the most costly. That's some of the most strategic, uncensored truth I'm hoping to communicate to you. Please believe me.

"BUT I WASN'T GONNA EAT IT. I WAS JUST GONNA TASTE IT."

—WINNIE THE POOH

Chapter

23

CHEW AND SPIT
ROMANCE

C.S. LEWIS GIVES US AN INCREDIBLE ANALOGY on the whole subject of

sex. He says that the Christian attitude towards sex is not that there is

anything wrong with sexual pleasure, as long as it's inside the marriage

covenant. He reasons that there's nothing wrong with enjoying sex,

any more than enjoying the pleasure of eating great food.

But a truly Christian perspective also says that you must not isolate

sexual pleasure and try to get it by itself any more than you would

try to get the pleasures of taste without swallowing and digesting

your food. In other words, it would be ridiculous if someone chewed   *Sounds gross! It is!*

food, enjoyed the taste temporarily, and then spit the food back out

again. (Got the picture? I'm sitting at a local restaurant right now, and

honestly, I'd get pretty freaked if the people at the next table started

chewing their food and then spitting it back out on the floor!)

What's that got to do with God's perspective on sex? (Everything.)

Let me ask you a really important question. Ready?

BY THE WAY YOU HANDLE
RELATIONSHIPS, ARE YOU
A "CHEW AND SPIT" PERSON?

Gross thought, isn't it? There is something pretty disgusting about a

person who says, "I just want to taste this food, but this digestion stuff

isn't important to me!" Yet I think that a similar thing is taking place

when a person says, "I want to pursue this relationship sexually, but

I'm not interested in waiting until marriage." We're basically saying,

"I want to enjoy the taste and the pleasure of this activity without making this person a permanent part of me." We often don't want any "digestive responsibilities." We just want to "taste" and then throw the person to the floor. That's where I get my crazy title, "Chew and Spit Romance."

From my perspective, our society has countless "chew and spit" sexual encounters. And God takes a really dim view of them. How do I know? Well, listen to what He says in Hebrews 13:4 (NIV). It's pretty uncensored, if you ask me:

> FROM A **BIBLICAL** PERSPECTIVE, THE PLEASURE OF SEXUAL INTIMACY IS **ONLY** TO BE "TASTED AND ENJOYED" INSIDE THE **ONENESS** OF THE **MARRIAGE** COVENANT.

"Marriage should be honored by all and the marriage bed kept pure. For God will judge the adulterer and all the sexually immoral."

|Ouch.| Ever been judged by God? It doesn't sound like a happy picture.

From a biblical perspective, the pleasure of sexual intimacy is only to be "tasted and enjoyed" inside the oneness of the marriage covenant. Joshua Harris has a great story about one of his own experiences that relates to all of this. Let me re-cap part of it for you.

Josh was doing radio interviews by phone about one of his relationship books. Normally, the interviews were with Christian radio stations. So it was a little like being interviewed by Mr. Rogers. ("It's a beautiful day in the neighborhood!")

The interview I'm talking about, though, was with a secular station in Tampa, Florida. Josh was put on hold before the interview went on the air. Music played from the station as he was waiting. Instead of hearing Point of Grace, he realized that he was hearing Metallica. (His thoughts? "Give me back Mr. Rogers!")

The secular radio station host came on the air, and I believe the exact first words out of the guy's mouth were, "Oh, my *#&%! They tell me you're still a *virgin!* Is that really true?"

Josh answered back, "Virgin with a capital 'V.'"

So the guy answers, "But what if you get married and find out that the girl is terrible in bed?"

Josh's answer? "Well, I won't have anything to compare it with, will I?"

A girl host chimes in at this point. "That's a great answer!" she says.

"Seriously, man," the radio guy continues. "What happens if you get married and she's terrible in bed?"

Joshua Harris, in his normal candid style, responded something like this:

"Wait a minute. You've pinpointed a key problem in our society. We've made sex a performance sport. Why don't we just break out the Olympic scorecards? Besides that, what's going to happen if you marry someone who is good in bed and then one day, they're *not* good anymore?"

The radio guy blurted out, "I'll cheat!"

What was the radio host's problem? Ultimately, he didn't have a relationship with Christ. But from my vantage point, he was just another "chew and spit" guy. Sex was nothing sacred or deeply meaningful to him. It was just a self-centered, temporary pleasure with no responsibilities attached.

Way to go, God!

Since God authored sex, let me give you another snapshot of His perspective: "There's more to sex than mere skin on skin. Sex is as much a spiritual mystery as a physical fact. As written in Scripture,

'The two become one.' Since we want to become spiritually one with the Master, we must not pursue the kind of sex that avoids commitment and intimacy, leaving us more lonely than ever—the kind of sex that can never 'become one.'" (1 Cor. 6:16,17 MSG.)

Pretty clear, wouldn't you say?

So, let me ask you: Do you have relational integrity, or are you just another "chew and spit" person?

One more thing. No fair wanting to one day marry someone who is "new furniture" when you yourself are in the "antiquing business." And that, my friend, is the uncensored truth.

WHEN DEALING
WITH PAIN,
CHOOSE TO BE
THE VICTOR,
NOT THE VICTIM.

Chapter

24

GUY MEETS GUY; GIRL MEETS GIRL

SO YOU SNUCK TO THIS CHAPTER and hope that no one sees you read-

ing it. I'm really sorry. It shouldn't be that way.

I'm sad that the church world does such a rotten job of commu-

nicating on homosexual and lesbian tendencies. We seem to go to

one of two extremes. We either preach so hard against sin that people

who are struggling in this area feel like they have to go "under-

ground," or we awkwardly ignore the whole discussion. Even worse,

we make "gay jokes" and then wonder why people struggling in this

arena have so much hesitancy to turn to the church.

You're not alone!

I've been privileged to connect closely with many young men

and women who found themselves struggling to solidify their sexual

identity. Even as I write these words, I pray that Jesus will send this chapter as hope and understanding to incredible individuals who might need it. So though I am a million miles from an expert on this subject, allow me to share a few "bottom lines." It's my honest hope that my candor could be helpful to a few of you who are desperate for some answers but have nowhere to turn.

01. **Yes, I believe the Bible does clearly tell us that same-sex relationships are sin.** I think that's Scripturally very clear. But once again, Christ sincerely loves the person, even though He is brokenhearted over the sin.

02. **No, I don't believe that people are "born gay."** I do, however, believe *Very common misconception* that some people are wired personality-wise in a fashion that makes it easier for them to lean in that direction. Children pop out of their mom's womb with different temperaments and sensitivities. Thus, though I deeply believe that children are not "born gay," I do think some people find it easier to fall into homosexual patterns than others.

I think the same thing could be said of nearly any sin pattern we could mention. I, myself, have a very "everything or nothing" personality, which makes me an easy candidate for serious alcoholism. No, I've not allowed that to happen. I choose not to drink alcohol at all. But I realize that my personality-bent makes me an easy target for compromise in that area. In like manner, I think some personalities are an easier target for homosexual compromise.

03. **Just because you have had same-sex fantasies (or even compromised in a same-sex relationship) does not mean you are gay.**

The Word of God talks about how fear can be used by the enemy to tie us to something negative in our lives. ("The thing I greatly feared has come upon me" Job 3:25 NKJV.) That's why it's so crucial to break this fear focus. Please allow yourself to breathe a deep sigh of relief. Those feelings and temptations do not have to seal your future destiny. Only your choices will do that.

Titus 3:3 talks about this

But what if you found those same-sex relationships secretly pleasurable? Once again, the enemy attempts to energize all forms of sin in our lives. Your emotional and sensual reactions to those moments do not determine if you are gay. Only your personal, daily choices do that.

Let's use me for example. Let's pretend that I decided to go out drinking one weekend so I could forget about my pressures. Maybe I even enjoyed the experience so much that I wound up going home that night really plastered. (My friends are now laughing at the thought of how I would act drunk!) At any rate, none of that would make me an alcoholic. Not my choice that night. Not even my secret enjoyment. Only my repeated choice to give in to that pattern would make me an alcoholic. The parallels are obvious. So stop listening to the enemy's lies. On the other hand, realize that every single time you give into temptation, the enemy's stronghold in your life tightens its grip.

04. **A person is born neither totally homosexual nor totally heterosexual** (though obviously, the male or female sexual identity is clearly established at birth). In truth, human sexuality is a little more like a balance scale. That balance scale is affected by your natural temperament like we already said. But all sorts of life experiences (both positive and negative) also help to lean that scale further in one direction or another. That's why certain factors in your upbringing or painful rejections can make this whole issue worse. Life, through various circumstances, seems to lean your balance scale more heavily towards one side or the other. As always, though, Christ gives you the ultimate power to determine the outcome of those circumstances.

A lot sure has changed

Years ago, healthy American families were the bedrock for stable sexual development. Dads and moms worked together to create a loving, secure environment for their children. This kind of consistency and role-modeling made it easy for the balance scale to develop and tip in the appropriate direction. Unfortunately now, families are often splintered and unhealthy. Their positive impact on the development of a healthy sexual identity is often watered down, at best. Like one teenager told me recently, "Watching Bill Cosby on TV was the only way I figured out how a real man is supposed to act."

05. **We live in an over-sexed world.** It's little wonder that such a high percentage of today's youth culture struggles with sexual balance and purity. With constant images on the media and the Internet glorifying same-sex relationships, fantasy-driven temptation is at an all-time high. Suggestive same-sex images line the walls of almost every contemporary clothing store and flaunt sensuality in order to sell their clothing. So with all these influences, why would we be surprised by a rise in sexual identity issues? We're unisexing everything.

06. **If you have ever been taken advantage of by someone in your life when you were younger, the mind games can be especially huge.**

Please know that those mind games are just that—only mental games energized by the enemy to try to throw you off track. Whatever happened was not your fault. Yes, some painful memories and baggage may probably remain. But Christ wants to be way bigger than all that junk in your life. You alone decide if you are a victim or a victor.

On the other hand, don't be secretly frightened if a part of you found some of those earlier experiences more pleasurable than you want to admit. Again, this is just another deception of the enemy. You are not gay. Your pleasure came from a sense of emotional closeness and from the enemy's sexually-charged trap at the moment. Refuse to believe the secret lies he whispers in your mind.

07. **Again, I'm so sorry. The Church's unwillingness to "roll up our sleeves" and help sincere people with this challenge leaves them isolated, lonely, and very vulnerable.** Oftentimes, we force individuals to suffer silently with absolutely no help or support from any Christians around them. Unlike people struggling with many other vulnerabilities, they feel that they can tell no one nor reach out for help. They quietly remain isolated and vulnerable without Christ-honoring friendship or support.

Thus, it is easy to understand why some of these sincere
individuals slowly let the lies of the enemy become louder and
louder in their own minds.

For real—as a gift to you

That's probably why Christ had me write this short chapter to
you—so you could hear Christ's truth in place of the deafening lies that scream inside your mind.

Let me give a few loving suggestions to my friends who might find
themselves in this painful dilemma:

01. Again, realize that Christ had
me write this short chapter
as a love note to YOU. Cheesy

He knows the lies in your head

as it might sound, He wants
you to read every one of these

> REFUSE TO BELIEVE
> THE SECRET LIES
> HE WHISPERS
> IN YOUR MIND.

words as His attempt to break
through the lies you have been fearing in your own mind.
You are not gay. Yes, the awkwardness and temptations may
be there. Yes, you may have even given in to this temptation
before. But please realize that these circumstances in themselves do not make you a homosexual or a lesbian. I have
many, many amazing spiritual friends who have experienced
everything we are talking about. But they have chosen to fan

the positive, Christ-honoring desires and voices in their lives. And as a result, they live an incredibly fulfilled, happy life today of sexual wholeness and freedom.

02. **Read carefully all of the chapters in Uncensored dealing with freedom from sexual temptation.** The same principles that bring freedom in one area sexually will support freedom for you. Be especially aware of the strength of God's Word to bring growing power and wholeness to you. All along the journey, keep choosing to "feed your faith and doubt your doubts."

03. **Be especially honest with yourself about the impact of media on your life.** Only you will be able to accurately know your personal fuse-shorteners. But person after person has shared with me that their struggle became much more agonizing as they fanned it via the Internet, certain movies, magazines, etc.

04. **If a same-sex relationship becomes secretly appealing to you, have the self-discipline to distance yourself from that relationship.** Try to avoid spending long amounts of time together, being alone, taking trips alone, etc. Use the same common-sense guidelines you would use if you found yourself attracted to a person of the opposite sex and wanted to walk in purity. Whatever

you do, <u>do not discuss or even hint</u> to that person about your possible feelings of attraction.

Try not to let the enemy bring this topic to your mind often. When Satan does bring it up, mentally answer him with a Scripture

> **WHATEVER A MAN CONTINUES TO THINK ABOUT, HE SLOWLY BECOMES.**

like, "Greater is He that is in me than he that is in the world" (1 John 4:4 KJV). Remember that whatever you focus on, you fuel. So try not to give the enemy much "fuel" in this arena. Don't feel that you need to date or marry someone to "prove that you're OK." <u>Some of the healthiest people I know live such full lives that they are presently choosing to neither date nor marry.</u> *For real!* That's absolutely A-OK! Don't buy into this culture's twisted value system. You're fine as an individual. You don't have to be "locked at the hip" to someone else to be viewed as normal. At the right time, God will bring someone into your life if marriage is a desire He fans in your heart.

Get busy creating a life of purpose, friendship, and fulfillment for yourself. Put your emotional and mental focus on the positive, Christ-honoring things in life. Don't let this subject or secret fear consume you. Remember? The Bible says that "Whatever a man continues to think about, he <u>slowly</u> becomes." (Prov. 23:7, author's paraphrase.) So get your mind busy in different directions.

05. **Prioritize wholehearted participation in a healthy church family.** Many of your emotional, friendship, and spiritual needs will be met while enjoying the fun and the fulfillment of great Christian friends. Remember: "The <u>lone</u> ranger is often a <u>dead</u> ranger." So don't try to do the Christian life alone.

Most of all, remind yourself often that Jesus loves you so much that He prompted me to slip this chapter into this book. <u>It wasn't a part of my original writing outline.</u> But the Lord so badly wanted you to know that you're OK and that you're not locked into a gay life-style that He prompted me to write this. Read all the other chapters in this book carefully. Many of them (not just the sexual ones) will relate to your life.

He loves you

Please allow this chapter to be a private love gift from Jesus to you. I mean that so sincerely. It's no coincidence that you stumbled onto this book. Jesus so deeply loves and believes in you, in His most uncensored way.

MY PRESENT
CONDITION IS A
RESULT OF MY
PAST DISCIPLINES.
TODAY I CHOOSE
MY FUTURE.

—CHRIS CAPEHART

THE LIST: 13 WAYS TO BEAT TEMPTATION

 01. Accept personal responsibility for moral purity.

There's a prayer that I'm not sure God usually answers. This is how it goes, "Lord, take away all this sexual temptation!" I think He usually leans over from heaven and says, "*You* take away the things in your life that invite that temptation."

My point is simple. I think we've got to begin our commitment to sexual purity with the clear realization that we are going to have to continually make personal decisions that move us in that direction. The uncensored truth is that no matter how much you love God, you and He are going to have to be a team on this purity business. Sorry. There just isn't an easy, cheap way out.

You lose when you stop fighting

02. Recognize and immediately begin to remove fuse-shorteners in your romantic life. Remember that term earlier in the book? Fuse-shorteners are those places, people, and patterns that shorten your sexual fuse either physically or emotionally, making you more vulnerable to sexual temptation. That's why I often ask friends who are pursuing moral purity to list their own unique fuse-shorteners. We all have them.

Try taking a minute and listing some of yours below. If you're too embarrassed to write the whole word out, just use initials! You'll know what you mean. I'll give you a few possible examples to get you started:

Possible Fuse-Shortener PLACES:

• The back several rows at the movies

• The family room couch with John after everyone else goes to bed

• Parties that Josh and Rita throw

Possible Fuse-Shortener PEOPLE: (Listing friends and people here makes them neither "bad" nor "good." It's just being mature enough to realize that different people create different chemistry in our lives.)

- People who make a big joke of my values (like Suzanne)

- Ben and Kristina on a double-date (As couples, we deal with the same weaknesses.)

- The guys I used to party with.

Possible Fuse-Shortener PATTERNS:

- Being alone in the house or car with Clint after 10 P.M.

- Prolonged French kissing

- Spending time alone with Lynn when I'm really tired and my defenses are down

- Being on the Internet past 9 at night in my bedroom alone, especially when I have no specific purpose for my browsing.

Remember as you pinpoint your fuse-shorteners that there is usually nothing wrong with the specific place, person, or pattern itself. It's just important that you realize that your "sexual fuse" is slowly being shortened and closer to "igniting" when you mess around with these things. The uncensored truth is that we don't really "fall" into sexual temptation. Instead, we make small, consistent choices that slowly lead us in that direction.

03. Remember that SMALL compromises eventually lead to BIG trouble.
The point at which you violate your conscience, no matter how small, is where the "sexual snowball" starts down the mountain. Moral purity is so much easier when you internally stop yourself early in the game, instead of pushing all the limits. And remember, because of the "Law of Forbidden Fruit," this kind of self-control only makes you more attractive to the opposite sex, not less. So if you want people of the opposite sex to be tripping over you, this is a big key for long-haul victory.

04. Be honest with yourself regarding the influence of music, media, and the Internet in your life. OK, so this is a touchy area and people usually get pretty ticked when it is mentioned. But can *Please read with an open mind* I just point out that probably our quick defensiveness tells us more about the truth of this statement than anything else.

Obviously, everyone is going to have different standards and responses. But MTV, Hollywood, and the music industry aren't making billions of dollars every single month without becoming experts at youth and young-adult mindsets. Let me give you another interesting fact. Before Lucifer got kicked out of heaven, he was the worship leader there! Wild, isn't it? I think the devil was into music back then and still is today.

So here's a personal challenge. Consider removing heavy, non-Christian music from your life for only one month and replacing it with some Christian music you like. (There are thousands of artists to choose from. Just go to a Christian bookstore and spend some time listening to find some artists you connect with.) The simple "test" is to see what happens in your own life and heart if you focus on listening primarily to Christian music during this time period. At the end of those thirty days, ask yourself if your ability to cultivate moral and mental purity is higher or not. I think you'll be pretty blown away by the huge impact music has on your whole life.

*Simple test-
Life-changing results*

All forms of media and the Internet carry staggering influence in your pursuit of purity. No one can make those decisions for you but you. I can only tell you that they are far too important to ignore or determine by playing "follow the leader."

05. Never lower yourself to defraud another person.

"Defraud"—It's not exactly a term you throw around in everyday conversation. But it's used in the Bible to mean "arousing sexual desire in another person that you cannot righteously fulfill outside of marriage." With that definition in mind, we have some pretty clear guidelines:

REALIZE THAT YOUR BRAIN IS YOUR MOST POWERFUL SEX ORGAN.

- Don't defraud with your mouth by using language and promises to get what you want out of another person.

- Don't defraud with your clothes by dressing in a way that creates an invisible billboard on your chest reading, "Open for business."

- Don't defraud with your romance by pushing someone "over the cliff" sexually and then wondering why they can't stop in "mid-air."

- And on and on it could go…

Just call this section "Defrauding Unlimited!" It may be a really old term, but its everyday reality is about as contemporary as you get. Take a lesson from the household tack: "He never goes too far because he always uses his head!"

06. **Realize that your brain is your most powerful sex organ.** So work to control your thought-life. The Bible calls this whole process

"bringing your thoughts into captivity." It's a cheesy analogy but a relevant one. You can mentally visualize calling the cops on your negative thoughts and having them thrown into jail!

Let me give you a few suggestions on this vital area of controlling your thought-life:

• **Garbage in; garbage out.** In other words, don't listen to and watch a bunch of sexually charged media and then wonder why your thought-life reads like a script from *Sex & the City*.

• Don't pull the weeds without planting the flowers. Let me translate this "Mayo-ism" for you. I'm simply saying that you will never get rid of trashy thoughts in your head without purposefully choosing to replace them with positive ones. Sing Christmas carols if you have to! Just mentally choose to push the negative, sexual thoughts out of your mind and then strategically choose something positive to think about in their place. Obviously, Scripture is the most powerful replacement. Your grandma really was right: "An idle mind IS the devil's workshop."

• **Avoid freaking out when, after honest attempts at mental self-discipline, you still experience crazy, sexual thoughts**

racing through your mind. Adopt the philosophy of my wise, godly husband: "I can't stop the birds from flying over my head, but I can prevent them from building a nest in my hair!"

07. **Prioritize putting God's Word inside of you. It's the world's best "detergent"!** Have you ever heard of a guy in the Bible named David? (Remember? He's the kid who fought and killed a giant with a sling. Pretty cool, wouldn't you say?) At any rate, good old David messed up plenty in his life, including lots of sexual failures. Finally, almost in desperation, he cried out to God and said, "How does a young man cleanse his way?" Then he answers himself and says, "By taking heed according to [God's] Word" (Psalm 119:9 NKJV). See, even great men of God like David struggled with this area of sexual purity. But his big key to righteousness focused on getting the Word of God inside of himself.

Your same question

Your same answer

Be sure to look over the "Ammunition Scriptures" I give at the end of this chapter. Consider saying them out loud to yourself every morning and evening for several days (weeks). Little by little, these scriptures will become an exciting change-agent in your internal life. I can't explain it, but I promise it works. Give it a try. God's reputation is on the line, so it's a sure thing.

08. Visualize the shame, disappointment, and consequences that giving in to this area of temptation might bring to you and to those you care about. Wow! Have the guts to honestly try this one. It will be sobering but really helpful if you're completely honest with yourself. Remember my earlier quote? "You're free to disobey the commandments of God but never free to avoid the consequences." Nothing feels quite as amazing as a clean conscience.

On the other hand, try visualizing yourself telling a parent or coach that you are dropping out of school to raise a kid. Try seeing yourself walking down the school hall on the Monday morning after "the weekend when you gave it all." You catch him (her) talking with some close friends at the locker, looking pretty secretive. You can't help but wonder (though it's denied) if *you* were the topic of that secretive conversation. Just remember:

EASY DATES ARE NOT KEEPERS. THEY ARE JUST A TEMPORARY FIX UNTIL THE RIGHT ONE COMES ALONG.

09. Decide whether you want to be a long-term or short-term investor in the "First National Bank of Romance." When I was dating my husband, a night late in our engagement stands out vividly in my mind. We were deeply in love and weeks away from our wedding. Both our excitement and our hormones were at a pretty frenzied high. One evening, our romantic fervor got the best of us. Though we didn't "go all the way," it was quite clear that the tenor of the night was not heading towards "Nearer My God to Thee."

Finally, after some long and pretty impassioned kissing, I whispered to him, "Let's put the rest of this night 'in the bank.' We can pull it back out after we're married. Right now, let's just wait and let it 'collect some interest.'"

The expression might sound a little weird to you, but my amazing husband-to-be knew exactly what I meant. We were both determined to be <u>long-term investors</u> in the "Bank of Romance." You see, romance and sexuality work a lot like finances in one simple way. If you put your money in the bank and pull it out quickly, you won't have many dividends. If, on the other hand, you decide to invest your money as a long-term investor and then wait to withdraw it, your dividends will always be much higher. The only difference between the two strategies is time—basically your willingness to wait for a while until you "collect." Take the low road, and the rewards will be short-lived and minimal. But take the high road, and you're positioning yourself to be a very rich person relationally.

Let me mention one other thing related to long-term investing. The more intimately you care about a person and the more you desire the relationship to go the distance, the more important it is that you take things slowly. If the other person puts pressure on you not to wait, realize that this should be *Blunt but true* a huge "red flag." A willingness to be loose morally now is a clear sign that they will be willing to be loose later.

10. **Ask yourself the question, "What am I saving to give away to someone when I finally reach the point of wanting to spend the rest of my life with him/her?"** Did you get that question? It's so foreign to most of us that you probably will need to go back and read it again.

But stop here and think about it. What are you going to give away romantically to someone when you are certain that you want to marry him or her? I mean, airlines have certain privileges reserved for their frequent flyers called "Priority Status."

It would just make sense that we reserve some special privileges for the person we someday choose to marry. Instead, we often cheapen ourselves by giving away our "priority status" too easily.

GIRLS ARE ESPECIALLY DUMB IN THIS ARENA

(I'm a girl so I can say that!)

Here's a list of stupid things girls often believe that keep them from being long-term investors when out with a short-term guy:

- He's different with me.

Females: Read this!

- I'm going to change him.

- It really was the last girl's fault.

- I'm the only one he's done this with.

- He's really serious about me and ready to settle down.

- This is all OK because God put us together.

- Without me, he's never going to be all he could be.

- Other people just don't really understand him like I do.

As a high school and college student, I was sure of one thing: I wasn't going to give away my body. With God's help, I was determined to save that for marriage. (If you've already done that, remember again that "God never consults your past to create your future." In other words, ask Him for His forgiveness and start creating a "Chapter 2" in your life. Jesus loves you so much that He's honored to help you start all over when you ask for His help.)

It was also a really conscious decision on my part about how far I was going to let even my future husband go sexually. But I made another strategic, personal decision—one that only Jesus, my best girlfriend, and myself knew about. Since

I wasn't going to give a guy my body outside of marriage, I decided that I would save the words *"I love you"* for my future husband. Sound pretty cheesy? It really wasn't.

The night I said "I love you" to Sam Mayo, I was internally saying, "I've thought this thing through long and hard. And if you ask me, I'll marry you." Now let me issue a big warning: I HAD NOT TOLD HIM THAT! (In other words, I wasn't stupid enough to say, "Big boy, when you hear the three magic words, we're on for life!")

But I can't tell you how awesome it was to know that I had saved those words in a culture that otherwise cheapens them pretty easily. People love orange juice, good haircuts, cute hamsters, *and* their future mates!

One other disclaimer: Suppose you've already given away those words (and maybe lots more) to people in your life. That doesn't count you out, my friend. Just ask the Lord for His help to draw a line in the sand and start over. Jesus will be really happy to help out. He's more excited about creating a wonderful future for you than you even are. After all, He has vested interest in you. He made you.

11. Forgive yourself and other key people in your life. Remember: Guilt, bitterness, resentment, and rejection are easy footholds for the enemy to stand on in your life. Like we said earlier, "Unforgiveness is like drinking a poison and then expecting someone else to die from it." Sometimes hurt and rejection will make you want to do stupid things to get back at people. Don't do it. You'll eventually regret it every time.

Also know that the enemy wants you to believe that you are a big loser because of past mistakes. Just realize that when you ask Christ to forgive you, you are truly forgiven of all the junk in the past. So forgive yourself—Jesus has! His Word says that after you sincerely ask for His forgiveness, Jesus throws your sins away into a sea as far as the distance between the east and the west. And just to make things clear to the enemy, I think He even posts a "No Fishing" sign there!

12. **Be one of those rare people who cultivates dignity and a sense of self-respect in your own life.** I know that saving yourself for marriage is not the "norm" these days. But who wants to just be the "norm" anyway? Cultivate a sense of dignity and self-respect. People will not respect you any more than you respect yourself. That's a "for sure."

Let me remind you of one of my favorite uncensored statements: "People who have gone too far sexually remind me of the sign on a department store sales table: 'Merchandise slightly used. Greatly reduced in price.'"

13. **View the fight for sexual purity to be one you expect to win, but one you can expect to fight for the rest of your life.** Sound discouraging? It really isn't. Sex is just such a powerful force in our culture

that simple common sense tells you that if you're not on guard, the traps could be pretty frequent. But I want you to know that every choice you make to fight for purity will be rewarded one thousand times over. And one day, the rewards will come from unexpected places—like they did for me yesterday.

One of my adult sons was home for a couple of weeks before taking a job in L.A. He left me a note in my bedroom as he left for the airport. Now at age 25, guys aren't big note-writers to their moms. So I cherish every word. Let me close this chapter by telling you part of what he said to me:

"Thanks, Mom, for always having the guts and determination to live a life of integrity. I know it hasn't always been easy. But just know that I've noticed all your silent choices even when I didn't say anything. You have made me real proud to call you my 'Mum.' And by the way, I still think you're the best one in the universe! Love, Your Cool Son, Justin."

Sound like the pursuit of purity and integrity has been worth the fight? To me, it sure has. I'm not sure you could put any price on the value of that kind of relationship with your future children. So, let me encourage you, start earning those words now. ♡

SCRIPTURE AMMO TO FIGHT TEMPTATION

BANG!

(These are not direct quotations from the Bible but are para-phrased faith-statements based on the Scriptures. Use them to help strengthen you from the inside out.) Try reading some of your favorites out loud a couple of times a day for a few weeks. It will change everything! Even better, put your favorites on index cards. Then carry them around with you and/or post them in visible spots (like your bathroom mirror) where you will see them often.

01. *No, despite all these things, overwhelming victory is mine through Christ, who loves me.* (Romans 8:37 NLT)

02. *No test or temptation that comes my way is beyond the course of what others have had to face. All I need to remember is that God will never let me down; he'll never let me be pushed past my limit; he'll always be there to help me come through it.* (1 Corinthians 10:13 MSG)

03. *I am with you; that is all you need. My power shows up best in weak people.* (Jesus' words—2 Corinthians 12:9 TLB)

04. *For whatever is born of God overcomes the world; and this is the victory that has overcome the world—my faith.* (1 John 5:4 NASB)

05. *I choose to resist the devil. Thus, according to the Word, he must flee from me.* (James 4:7 NASB)

06. *The God of peace will soon crush Satan under my feet.* (Romans 16:20 TLB)

07. *You are from God, little children, and have overcome them; because greater is he who is in you than he who is in the world.* (1 John 4:4 NASB)

08. *Happy is the man who doesn't give in and do wrong when he is tempted, for afterwards he will get as his reward the crown of life that God has promised those who love him.* (James 1:12 TLB)

09. *And I pray that Christ will be more and more at home in your hearts as you trust in Him. May your roots go down deep into the soil of God's marvelous love. And may you have the power to understand, as all God's people should, how wide, how long, how high, and how deep His love really is.* (Ephesians 3:17, 18 NIV)

10. *And I am convinced and sure of this very thing, that He Who(began) a good work in me will(continue)until the day of Jesus Christ [right up to the time of His return], developing [that good work] and perfecting and bringing it to full completion in me.* (Philippians 1:6 AMP)

11. *I cried out, "I'm slipping!" but your unfailing love, O LORD, supported me.* (Psalm 94:18 NLT)

12. *Now, all glory to God, who is able to keep me from falling away and will bring me with great joy into his glorious presence without a single fault.* (Jude 24 NLT)

13. *The angel of the LORD encamps around those who fear him, and he delivers them.* (Psalm 34:7 NIV)

14. *For You are my hiding place; You protect me from trouble. You surround me with songs of victory.* (Psalm 32:7 NLT)

15. *Have you never heard? Have you never understood? The LORD is the everlasting God, the Creator of all the earth. He never grows weak or weary. No one can measure the depths of his understanding. He gives power to the weak and strength to the powerless. Even teenagers will become weak and tired, and young men will fall in exhaustion. But those who trust in the LORD will find new strength. They will soar high on wings like eagles. They will run and not grow weary. They will walk and not faint.* (Isaiah 40:28-31 NLT)

16. *I must be prepared. I am up against far more than I can handle on my own. I will take all the help I can get, every weapon God has issued, so that when it's all over but the shouting, I'll still be on my feet.*
(Ephesians 6:13 MSG)

17. *I will not fear, for You are with me. I will not anxiously look around, for You are my God. You will strengthen me, surely You will help me. Surely You will uphold me with Your righteous right hand.* (Isaiah 41:10 NASB)

18. *For God is at work within me, helping me want to obey him, and then helping me do what he wants.* (Philippians 2:13 TLB)

19. *Now I am free from the power of sin and I am a slave of God, and (his benefits to me include holiness and everlasting life.)* (Romans 6:22 TLB)

Great verses!

20. *I am convinced that nothing can ever separate me from his love. Death can't, and life can't. The angels won't, and all the powers of hell cannot keep God's love away. My fears for today, my worries about tomorrow, or where I am—high above the sky, or in the deepest ocean—nothing will ever be able to separate me from the love of God demonstrated by my Lord Jesus Christ when he died for me.* (Romans 8:38, 39 TLB)

SOME PERSONAL WORDS OF CLOSING FROM JEANNE TO YOU

from my heart

It's the 4th of July and I'm sitting on my porch, doing the final edits for UNCENSORED before it goes to the printer. I want to take a minute to thank you for letting me make this journey with you. What a great ride it's been!

Ground zero of my heart right now is to help youth leaders be more effective in really connecting with today's youth culture. If you're interested in that, please check out my Web site at www.youthleaderscoach.com. I also have a MySpace page. It would be really fun to hear from some of you. So sorry, though, I don't have enough hours in the day to answer questions. But it would be great to connect more personally with you. You can find me at http://www.myspace.com/jeannemayo.

There's a guy named Robert Frost, the author of one of my favorite poems called, "The Road Less Traveled." It pretty accurately describes the relational lifestyle I'm challenging you to consider. The poem is about a guy who is taking a walk in a wooded area when he comes to a fork in the road and has to choose between two different pathways. One is a smooth, well-worn path that lots of other people have obviously taken. And then there's a second road that is not nearly as cleared and easy to travel. It looks like very few people have ever paid the price to take that pathway. The guy stands at the fork in the road, trying to make his decision.

Let me close with the last part of the poem:

> "I shall be telling you this story with a sigh
>
> Somewhere ages and ages hence.
>
> Two roads diverged in a wood
>
> And I took the one less traveled by
>
> And that has made…
>
> All the difference."

Thanks for being the gutsy kind of traveler who now considers the relational "road less traveled." I'm not saying the "UNCENSORED Road" is an easy one. Truth be told, it's not the road for weak, spineless people. But it's the one that will ultimately open the doors to the most fulfilling life imaginable.

And so, my friend, here's my challenge to you. Don't go where the easy, well-worn relational path may lead. Instead, have enough guts to go where your friends really haven't made much of a path before. And leave a trail.

You now stand at the fork in a pretty important road. Please…take the one "less traveled."

Cheering You On,

Jeanne

THE INVITATION OF A LIFETIME

DO YOU REMEMBER HOW YOU FELT on Christmas morning when you were a little kid? The excitement was just too much to handle! I remember getting up early, sneaking downstairs to look at all my wrapped gifts, and then bombarding my parents' bed so they would "get up and start to open the presents!"

Most of those gifts were short-lived. I mean, the bikes eventually rusted and the other toys quickly fell apart. Truth be told, I eventually just lost interest in most of them.

There's really only one gift I've ever received that has weathered the ultimate test of time. And since this is an honest book about relationships, let me add another statement: There is only one rela- *For real...* tionship in the universe that has never disappointed me, never been too busy to deeply connect with me, and never left me with some gnawing emptiness on the inside.

That gift would be my personal relationship with Jesus Christ.

We make this whole thing about knowing Christ way too tough. It's not about what "religion" we are (or aren't), what clothes we wear, or how many great things in life we manage to pull off. Real relationship with Christ begins when we choose to sincerely ask Christ into our life to be our Best Friend, our Savior, and our Lord.

It's the "lordship" part that throws a lot of people off. You see, Jesus is kind of like my husband on this count. Sam Mayo doesn't want to be "*one* of Jeanne's husbands." He wants to be "*the* man" in my life. And wisely, Jesus Christ gave His life on the cross for you so He could earn the right to be "*the Man*" in your life. He doesn't want "a piece of the pie." He wants the whole thing. He never asks for perfection. He knows we'll all mess up countless times. He just waits for an invitation from you to begin a personal, life-changing relationship with Him. And in John 10:10, He promises what that decision will bring you. He says, "I've come to the world to give LIFE—abundant life!"

Awesome promise!

So who knows? This book might wind up becoming more to you than just a blunt expose on relationships. I've prayed that somehow, some of my readers might sense Christ's love even as they browsed through these pages. Why? Like I've said over and over, *every human relationship will fall painfully short of meeting the deepest longings for intimacy buried inside you. Only through personal relationship with Jesus*

Christ can a true sense of purpose, unconditional love, and guidance for the future be captured.

If you're interested in starting on this incredible journey, think about praying something like this:

Jesus, I don't think I picked this book up by accident. I'm a million miles from being perfect; but people tell me that Your love is bigger than all the junk and mistakes in my life. Thanks for dying on the cross for me. What a gutsy, selfless act of friendship.

So, in simple, kid-like faith, I ask You to come into my life right now. I'm asking You, Jesus, to become my Best Friend, my Savior, and the Boss of my life. I can't promise perfection from this point on, but You know my heart. I really do want an authentic, personal relationship with You. So according to what the Bible teaches, this simple but heartfelt action now makes me "Your kid." By faith in Your Word, I now choose to believe that I am a new person—from the inside out. Help me as I begin this exciting journey of being an authentic Christ-follower. I pray this in Jesus' Name. Amen.

The simple prayer that Changes EVERYTHING

✕ ✕ ✕

I've prayed a prayer kind of like that with thousands of young adults and teenagers all over the globe. And believe me, it works! I promise. Even more strategic, let me say again that your personal relationship with Christ will become the single greatest relationship you can ever, ever cultivate. He alone can create the "Dream Relationship" that most all of our media fantasizes about.

And that, my friend, is the most important UNCENSORED truth you'll receive in your entire lifetime.

Lovingly Honored To Be In The Same "Family,"

Jeanne

If you prayed this prayer today and really meant it, please contact my publisher on the Web at **www.harrisonhouse.com** to receive a free book to help in your new walk with Christ. If you'd rather, you may write them at:

Harrison House Publishers

P.O. Box 35035

Tulsa, Oklahoma 74153

jeanne mayo's
youth**leader's**coach

www.youthleaderscoach.com

No one ever made it to the big game without a coach... So why tackle youth ministry without one?

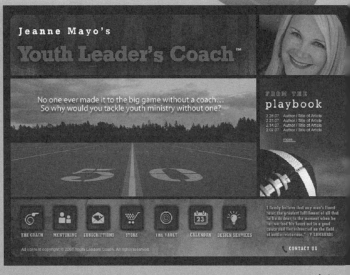

coaching
Jeanne's most valuable tools for winning the game... Monthly mentoring at its best!

the vault
Free youth leadership coaching shared by Jeanne and other premiere youth leaders from across the nation.

resources
Every great team needs the right equipment to succeed.

our forum
Interactive message board where youth leaders share ideas and events that actually work!

calendar
Jeanne speaks frequently across the nation and internationally to large youth gatherings and youth leadership forums. See when she is in your area.

for more information call us @ 404-284-8262

ABOUT THE AUTHOR

Acclaimed by *Ministries Today* as "America's Number One Youth Pastor," Jeanne Mayo has thrown her heart and passion into youth ministry for nearly four decades. Her ministry DNA is reflected in her life mission statement: "The motivation and mentorship of Kamikaze Christianity into practicing and potential Kingdom champions."

The years have seen incredible results. In Nebraska, she multiplied a group of a few dozen students into hundreds. Then in Illinois, she was met by a group of 30 students that grew to nearly 1,000 and a Christian school of 1,400. While in California, she had the privilege of developing a group of 90 students into over 500 in only one year's time. Currently, she and her husband are leading an incredible team in Atlanta, where amazing growth is happening once again.

Jeanne's successful ministry has placed her in high demand as a youth ministry and youth leadership communicator. She has criss-crossed the U.S. and the globe, speaking in countless venues to teenagers and college students, as well as their leaders. Now one of her greatest joys during these travels is to reconnect with some of her hundreds of spiritual sons and daughters in full-time ministry all over the world.

In recent years, Jeanne founded "The Youth Leader's Coach," a non-profit organization that seeks, "to instruct, equip, inspire, and encourage the youth pastors and youth leaders of this generation."

Through "The Youth Leader's Coach," Jeanne is now focusing on leaving a legacy for youth pastors and youth leaders of this generation. She is a coach, mentor, and "Big Sis" to youth leaders across the country. Jeanne is also pouring her heart into creating resources designed specifically for those influencing the lives of teenagers. She is a regular columnist for *Group Magazine* and *Ministries Today*. She most recently authored the popular leadership book, *Thriving Youth Groups*.

In response to Jeanne's achievements in youth and young adult ministry, Oral Roberts University awarded her a Doctorate of Divinity. Jeanne also sponsors her bi-annual *National Youth Leaders' Conference*. This widely acclaimed event has become one of the largest gatherings of its kind, drawing over 3,000 youth pastors and leaders from all fifty states and five foreign countries.

Jeanne found her way to the cross as a young teenage woman. After college, she married her "hero," Pastor Sam Mayo, who has been the senior pastor at most of the places she has served. Jeanne considers her most cherished accolade, however, to be that she is the proud mom of two adult sons, Josh and Justin. Jeanne's favorite quote comes from missionary Jim Elliot, which contains the words that motivate her to live out her life mission:

"He is no fool who gives what he cannot keep to gain what he cannot lose."

To contact Jeanne Mayo,

please write to:

"The Youth Leader's Coach"

P.O. Box 450309

Atlanta, Georgia 31145

Phone: 404.284.8262

Email: info@youthleaderscoach.com

Or visit her on the Web at:

www.youthleaderscoach.com

Tell us how UNCENSORED has changed your life.

Please visit **www.uncensoredbook.com**

ENDNOTES

1 National Center for Health Statistics.

2 Lookadoo, Justin and Hayley DiMarco, *Dateable,* (Grand Rapids, Michigan: Fleming Revell, 2004), p. 29.

3 Adapted from *Please Hear What I Am Not Saying,* Charles Finn, 1966, www.poetrybycharlescfinn.com.

4 Smith, David W., *Men without Friends,* (Nashville: Nelson Publishing, 1990), pp. 46-47.

5 Quiz adapted from *Relationships* by Drs. Les and Leslie Parrott (Grand Rapids, Michigan: Zondervan, 1998), pp. 195-196.

6 Parrott, Drs. Les and Leslie, *Relationships,* (Grand Rapids, Michigan: Zondervan, 1997), p. 153.

7 Study referenced in *The Friendship Factor* by Alan Loy McGinnis, (Minneapolis: Augsburg Publishing House, 1979), pp. 44-46.

8 Roberts, Ted, *Pure Desire,* (Ventura, Califorina: Gospel Light 1999).